Bobby Dazzler

A Rossendale Childhood

By Esther-Margaret Hood

Also by Esther-Margaret Hood:

Hong Kong Novels

A Man In Macau
Dragon Boat Café
Painting With Love

ISBN: 979-8682191598

In memory of Harry Spence, my friend.

"Near the snow, near the sun, in the highest fields,
See how these names are feted by the waving grass,
And by the streamers of white cloud
And whispers of wind in the listening sky."
(Stephen Spender).

Contents

Preface

"Real life is under no obligation to be convincing."
(Neil Gaiman)

It is quite difficult to recreate the world of a child –
that sense of wonder coupled with unquestioning
acceptance. When my known world collided with a
small, outdated Lancashire farm in the summer of
1959, I didn't turn my nose up at the lack of a tractor,
I thought a horse and cart were marvellous. I had
never been anywhere near a farm before, or even a
single cow, so, aged "nearly six", it was all an
adventure. Lucky, lucky me!

I rarely speak of Springhill Farm and the Spence
family who ran it. Every now and then, something
will crop up and I will make a remark which reveals
that I know a little about cattle. People are invariably
surprised – nobody equates me with farming, why
should they? And yet it was the experiences I had as a
child knocking about on a small farm in Higher
Cloughfold, Rossendale, that have had a substantial
influence on my life.

I have travelled and worked in various parts of the
world, but there have always been echoes of
Springhill, barely audible most of the time yet
insistent and getting ever louder as the years passed.

At one point, during a period of illness, I would listen to northern people being interviewed on television just to hear their voices – I would have little or no interest in what they were talking about!

In 2012, the London suburban house where I had lived whilst my two children were growing up had to be sold. The boys were adults now, it was time to pack my bags. Where to go? Rossendale. It was that simple and that complicated in one word. So, that summer, I took a week-long holiday in the area to see if I thought I could live there again – after all, I hadn't lived in Rossendale since 1964. After seven days, I made up my mind – I would do it. Friends and family alike were taken aback at this plan and persuaded me that if I was really set on the idea, I should rent a property for a while, rather than buy somewhere. I did. I found a little house to rent in the centre of Waterfoot and planned to live there whilst I found my feet. In October, I closed the front door of my southern house, the furniture had already gone and a taxi was waiting for me. I have never looked back.

I have no concerns about writing in so much detail about the Spence family. In fact, it is because they are all gone now, with hardly anyone to remember them, that I have felt compelled to record their lives. Harry Spence knew that I had attempted to write about the farm. I once even sent him an article which I had written to see if he would agree to it. In fact the article was not published, but I had the impression that he was a bit sorry about that!

My difficulties with ever trying to explain my life at Springhill, and the farm in particular, are perhaps best illustrated by a comment made by an older friend who read that same article.

She thought that I had written a story *for* a child not the story *of* a child - still less did it occur to her that the child was me!

"You will need to change it a bit though," she said. "Nobody was using a horse and cart in the 1960s – it was all tractors by then."

For years – decades – I would forget about the farm, but somehow it always came back, demanding that it shouldn't be forgotten, daring me to let it die. I found I couldn't do that.

Had I been older – or younger – it wouldn't have happened. By chance, I was exactly the right age. A door opened for me onto a world I didn't know and would never know again. A younger child could not have ventured into this land; older, I would have been too shy, bored or even embarrassed. But a curious five-year-old wasn't going to dither in the doorway. Oh no, I walked right on in! Sixty years on, I can appreciate just what an experience it was. By the time I was eleven, my family left the area and it was all over. Except it wasn't; my years at Springhill and my friendship with the Spence family have informed all my life.

One

Stepping Back

There's not a lot to Higher Cloughfold these days, but then there never was much. There's only one shop now plus a bus stop, a pub and a Baptist chapel all clustered round a bend in a road that comes from a small town and goes up to a village. Some cottages, of course, and an imposing house set back from the road amidst trees. In summer, the trees are so full the house, Springhill, is all but invisible. There was never any sign of a farm at Higher Cloughfold, but it was there: Springhill Farm, just round the back of the house. Its name was the grandest thing about it.

I spent many, many happy hours as a child at that farm: playing in the fields and round the yard, taking in the whole life of a small, mixed farm, and befriending the Spence family who ran it. I never forgot those days. As a family, we left Springhill in the winter of 1964; I was only eleven, but the experience lives with me still.

When I knew the Spences in the early 1960s, their family consisted of Mrs Spence and her three adult children, Harry, Billy and Betty. None of the three had married and they all still lived together in the end house of a small terrace just off Edge Lane in Higher Cloughfold. In 1959, aged five, I considered this to be the farmhouse, although it was certainly a long way from the more traditional idea of a farmhouse.

After we left Springhill, I had almost nothing to do with any of it. I called in at the farm two or three times in my teens, that was all. So, it was with some trepidation that in 2001, at the age of forty-seven, I found myself once again on Mrs Spence's doorstep. Mrs Spence would not be there, of course, she had died in 1974. Betty too had died some time in the early 1990s. But as far as I knew, Harry and Billy were both still around. I estimated that they would be in their seventies.

I had written and told them I would be coming. I knew I wouldn't get a reply, but that wasn't the point. The letter wasn't really for the benefit of Harry or Billy; what it actually did was force me to turn up – I would never have let them down. For added impetus, I took my two sons with me, curious to meet the fabled Harry!

We left the car on the Red Lion carpark and crossed Newchurch Road, walking along by the wall of Springhill House. I felt quite nervous; this was already turning into more of a challenge than I had anticipated. I looked over the wall at the stone-faced house. It had been cleaned to an unfamiliar sandy colour; when our family lived there, the stone was a deep blackish brown, testament to the Rossendale valley's industrial past. Now, cleaner air prevailed. Who lived at Springhill now I had no idea, but Harry was still at the farmhouse – where else would he be?

I stood quite still looking at Springhill House; it represented so much. And what did I think I was going to say to Harry anyway? This could all be a big mistake, I thought, there was still time to go straight back to the car and drive away. Leave the memories intact. But no, no, I couldn't back out now – the letter had seen to that.

The walk down the side of the Springhill garden wall was reassuringly familiar. Even so, I hesitated at the three stone steps up to the first cottage – "the farmhouse". This really might be a bad idea; forty years is a long time.

A dog inside sensed our presence and started to bark, then a man's voice and the door swung open. I didn't recognise the elderly man standing there, which was a shock in itself, but it must be him . . .

"Harry! Hello!"

"Don't mind dog. I've shut it up." He stood back as we came into the gloomy living room. "You don't like dogs, do you?"

I stared at him. "No, not much. Fancy you remembering that."

"I don't forget much. Well, I've nowt else to do but remember things."

As he moved into the room, lowering himself carefully into a tired armchair, it was all I could do not to wince. He was crippled with arthritis – I hadn't been ready for that. In my mind, Harry was still heaving milk churns about, tossing hay with a pitchfork, grappling with a wayward calf. Not this.

The room was dim, and as far as I could tell looked pretty much as it had all those years ago when Mrs Spence had ruled the roost. The room had the same white pot sink in the corner and a free-standing ancient gas stove, along with assorted pieces of long-past-it furniture.

10

"You knew I was coming then," I said. "I just assumed you got my letter."

"Oh, aye. Came last week."

I had known he wouldn't reply. As a child, I knew he could read – but writing? Well, probably, but possibly not much past a signature. I don't suppose he ever wrote much, not letters anyway.

I introduced him to my sons, Tom and George. "We thought it would be nice to see you," I ventured. "See how you are." Of course, I regretted this last remark as soon as it left my lips, but he didn't mind.

"This is how I am," he said. "Not much, is it? Can't hardly get out now."

"Do you get to the shops – or do you have things delivered?"

"Neighbour - Margaret - does it for me. She does mine when she's going for herself. Goes to Asda in Rawtenstall."

"Goodness, is there an Asda these days?"

"Oh aye – it's a big un an' all."

"Well, that's kind of her to do that for you."

He nodded. "It is. But I shouldn't have let her do it. Meant I didn't need to go out. Now, I can't go out even if I want to."

"But I suppose you have to take the dog out? Funny, I didn't imagine you having a pet. What's it called?"

"April."

"April?" I raised an eyebrow. "Doesn't sound like your sort of a name for a dog?"

"Oh, I know. It were called that when I got it. I want to get rid of it, but somebody wanted me to have

11

it for company. What do I want with an animal in a house?" Unexpectedly, he chuckled.

Suddenly, things felt easier. I was laughing with him. This was better. Harry with a pet! The idea was nonsense! We both knew it. And this had reminded me, also, of how he always described animals as "it". When I had first encountered this habit, I had thought it very odd, but I got used to it.

"So, when did you retire, Harry?"

"Is that what they call it? Retiring? I just give up like." He thought a moment. "It's a fair few years back. The council took the fields for a sports centre at Marl Pits. I still kept quite a few cows up on the moor for a while, but the grazing weren't good enough really. I got more sheep – remember us starting out with them? Just two in that shed in the Croft? I had more than a hundred by the time I give up."

"A hundred! Where on earth did you keep them?"

"They had to winter out. I couldn't keep that many on the yard. Always reared a few calves as well, you know. It were alright."

I nodded. "Alright" would be just about it, but I sensed there was something else going on here.

Harry appeared to be living in the house alone.

"So, what about Billy?" I asked. "Did he help with the sheep too?"

"No." Harry was surprisingly firm. "He left the house after mother died. We didn't speak for a long while even before she died. Don't speak now either," he said.

"Where is he then?" Well, I thought, that's a relief – at least Billy was still around somewhere.

"Don't know. Up the lane, in a caravan I think. He walks past every day."

"What – every day and you don't speak to him! What happened?"

"Ah, summat. Nowt worth talking about."

And that was that. I tried a few different approaches, but Harry was not to be drawn. Conversation about his brother was at an end.

"And Betty? What happened Harry? I heard she died, I lived in Hong Kong then, but I still heard."

"Aye, bad news don't stay shut up for long." His old eyes suddenly swam with tears. "She were ill. They couldn't do owt like."

Listening to him, I recalled clearly the way Harry used to change his manner of speaking when I was a child. With Billy, there had been an almost incomprehensible dialect; with other adults this was toned down and it became the style of speech I was following quite easily now. But when I was a little girl, he spoke to me correctly, grammatically, almost as if he didn't want me to speak in his local way. Not that I would have been allowed to! The very idea makes me smile.

"Going to have to move soon meself." Harry gestured at his legs. "Arthritis. I can't hardly get upstairs now."

"Is that being arranged, a move? Do you have a date?"

"Nah. Not yet. It'll be a while yet. Couple of years I reckon."

"I'm glad I came now then," I said, trying to inject a note of brightness, "I might never have found you."

13

He looked at me, the twinkle back in his eyes. "Oh, you would have found me. If anybody would, you would!"

Little by little, I teased some of my missing forty years out of him. I soon realised it was easier to work backwards.

So, what about the old farm buildings and the Crofts, those two small fields which edged right onto the yard? The cattle and all the rest of the livestock?

"The sheep all went at finish. I kept calves right to the end – but I couldn't lift the sacks of feed any more. That was when I had to give up. It were over like.

"The buildings are some houses now. Smart like. It were young Pickles took them over – you know, them from the shop."

I just nodded sadly. It seemed an awful way for everything to have ended like this. That solid family, struggling on in this house with that ramshackle farm and now just Harry, living out his life in this gloomy parlour with a dog he didn't want.

I stood up. The boys, who had been astonishingly still and silent, stood up too.

Harry nodded towards the old gateleg table. "See, there's some sweets in that table drawer. You two can 'ave 'em. Got them for you."

We found two packets of liquorice allsorts. I looked at Harry, surprised. "Has there always been a drawer in that table? Is it the same table?"

"Oh aye, it's same table – mother had a cloth over it. You couldn't see the drawer then."

"I'll be up in Lancashire some time next year, Harry. I'll let you know when," I said.

"I'll be here," he said. "Don't know about dog!"

Two

Springhill

Whilst Springhill is the actual house, in our family, the word has become synonymous with a period of time, a whole way of life. So that when I refer to Springhill, I am actually speaking of not just the house itself, but a stage in my life. A time which included so many things, well-remembered and not rose-tinted either. How much does a pre-teen remember? A lot!

The house itself is a big, stone-faced building, originally built in the mid-nineteenth century. It stands in a large garden, with big mature trees and rhododendron bushes. When we lived there, there was a large, oval lawn with a drive running right round it, but nowadays there is no lawn and the whole space in front of the house is tarmac and resembles a car park. A pity.

My family lived in the main part of the original house, accessed by the front door, just as it is now. I suspect that the similarity ends there.

Once through the front door, the insistent slow tick of a grandfather clock welcomed you into a mosaic tiled hallway – a wonderful coloured floor of gold, blue and red. It must have been quite dark in the hall – there are no windows there – but I don't remember it as particularly dim. The house telephone (Rossendale 2110) was there too. To the left, a door opened into a large, handsome lounge, while to the right was a square dining room with, a step or two further down the hall, a big kitchen behind it. If you carried on still further down the hall, past the bottom of the stairs, you turned left past the door to the cellar and came into another small room, which was used at various times as a bedroom.

The staircase, carpeted and with traditional brass rods, took you up to the first floor with its large bedrooms, and extraordinary bathroom. This was a luxury bathroom like no other and certainly not in keeping with a Victorian country house. It was fitted with a mint green suite with round, fat, shiny chrome taps. And the bath taps were not at one end of the tub as one might expect, but fitted into the side about halfway down. There wasn't a plug as I had previously understood bath plugs either, but more of a stopper that plunged up and down. That sort of fitting is quite popular nowadays, but in the early 1960s it was positively space age! Or, as I was to learn much later, positively Art Deco.

(I never told Harry about that luxurious bathroom; even at seven I sensed it would be unkind when he didn't have a bathroom at all.)

From the first floor, the staircase continued up to a second, attic floor. Two big rooms up there and a much smaller one, which was my first bedroom at Springhill. Later, I moved to one of the bigger rooms and sometimes now, passing the house, I look up at the window of that room just under the roof line, and think of my nine-year-old self gazing out.

17

In the winter, Jack Frost would make thick icy patterns on the glass – it makes me laugh these days when people talk about cold bedrooms. I could show them cold bedrooms! Heating that house must have been a nightmare. No central heating of course, and huge rooms with high ceilings. My father had a couple of Aladdin paraffin stoves which he placed optimistically on the turns in the staircase, but I can't say they made much difference. The main bedrooms had fireplaces, but they were never used in my time; we had some small electric fires up there.

The ground floor was a different matter. The kitchen boasted a large Aga – and this was long before anyone thought of rhyming it with saga. It stood on a base of terracotta tiles and the hotplates had heavy lids with twirly chrome handles. There was a top oven for cooking and also a bottom oven for warming plates. My Granny used to put Grandpa's slippers in the bottom oven when he was due home from work! This Aga was quite a workhorse and not a common appliance at the time - maybe it was installed by the same people who fitted the bathroom! It was lovely for warmth though; the kitchen was always welcoming when I came back from the farm.

The lounge had an open fireplace and when not lit we had a big electric fire in front of the grate. There were beautiful brocade curtains in that room and a thick plain green carpet. *(I didn't tell Harry about them either.)*

I rarely went in the cellar. It was accessed by a steep flight of stone steps and it was very cold down there. Even now I can get goose pimples thinking about that chill. It had been whitewashed at some stage and was lit by a couple of bare bulbs. There was nothing down there except some chemical apparatus which my grandfather had used for making a traditional ointment. He had had hopes of manufacturing this on a bigger scale, but nothing came of it. We didn't use the cellar as a store room, or anything of that sort, it was just a big, cold empty space under the house.

Springhill had been bought by my grandparents and over the years it was home to quite a number of family members, three possibly four generations. I remember the weddings of two of my aunts at Newchurch church and the receptions which followed on the Springhill lawn. My two youngest sisters were born there, we posed for photographs on the lawn and in front of the house on various occasions; Springhill was the hub of our family life and even now, as shorthand, those of us who are older still refer to it as a marker of events.

There is also a gatehouse, the Lodge, and after my youngest sister, Rachel, was born in 1961, my grandparents left the main house and went to live there.

Throughout my life, there have been echoes of Springhill. They pop up all the time – I've only to travel on the West Coast mainline from London to hear the announcement:

". . . no smoking in the carriages or the vestibules . . ."

Vestibule. Who uses a word like that these days? Well, apparently the passengers on the West Coast mainline, although somehow I doubt it! Until I started catching those trains, I hadn't heard the word in more than forty years. There is a vestibule at Springhill . . .

The vestibule at Springhill was like a grand – very grand – porch. It had stained glass windows set in varnished wooden doors with wrought iron handles, and sat directly in front of the main front door to the house. It was made of the same stone as the house with narrow side windows also of stained glass. The effect from inside was of multi-coloured light. From outside it was imposing. One time, sitting on the train after yet another announcement, I thought about the vestibule. Really, it could be almost considered a room in itself. The floor was made up of small tiles in a mosaic pattern with, centrally, a large doormat sunk into the surface. At one side stood a wrought iron umbrella and stick stand and on the other side was a table with an arrangement of dried flowers and grasses in a large vase. There was also a lacquered glove box, but it was empty. Nobody ever seemed to use it, and certainly not for gloves.

It occurred to me, as the train neared Stoke-on-Trent, that nowadays the vestibule would have shoes in it, but in those pre-central heating days, shoes were worn throughout the house, not left at the front door. My wellingtons for the farm were stationed firmly outside the back door with the milk crate.

Three

Nearly Six

In the summer of 1959, aged five ("nearly six"), several things happened in quick succession. First, my parents, sister Vanessa and I moved to Springhill from Whitton in Middlesex; second, my sister Rosemary was born at the house, and third, my Granny took me round to the farm. She had been born on a Rossendale farm, so she knew the score.

Harry was working up by the field gate. He had Diamond with the muck cart standing to one side while he emptied a wheelbarrow, but he put his big fork aside as we approached. He must have known my Granny quite well; I remember them having some cheery chat and of course, she introduced me to him. He was about six feet tall, with dark brown springy hair and a ready smile. In every way, he was very similar in style to Monty Don, the television gardening expert – I often think of that comparison, the same relaxed, easy manner and the very similar looks. Harry always wore knee-length wellington boots, with blue jeans and a long-sleeved shirt. (The sleeves were always rolled up to his elbows.) He must have been in his early thirties.

He lifted me onto Diamond's back – goodness it was high up! And that, I think, was the only time I ever sat on the carthorse. She wasn't for riding at all really, she was a very willing worker on Harry's farm and they made a great team!

Harry asked if I would like to come back about tea-time to watch the cows being milked. I was quite excited. He suggested wellingtons and Granny must have thought this was a good idea because I was kitted out that very afternoon!

It was all quite a thrill, I can't tell you, but I do recall being very puzzled by one aspect of all this. Harry was not a boy, he was a man. Children didn't call men by their Christian names in those days, it wasn't done. A man was either an uncle or he was Mr so-and-so. I wasn't sure I felt comfortable calling this man Harry – but there it was. I better get used to it.

I seem to have understood from the start that this farm was all about the cows. There were plenty of other animals, plenty of other things to do, lots and lots to keep an inquisitive five-year-old occupied. (I imagine with a new baby in our house, it may have been one reason for Granny taking me there!) But the cows and their immovable routine dictated the day – every day.

And so it started, my long, slow initiation into the ways of cows. Watching the milking, wide-eyed, and fascinated, I took it all in. Harry did most of the work; in those first, early days of my visits, he milked by hand, sitting on an ancient three-legged stool, gripping the milk pail between his knees. It was in the shippen at one of those tea-time milking sessions that I first met Billy, Harry's younger brother. (Another man you called by his Christian name!)

It seemed to me then that Billy was either there or he wasn't. You could never just tell. As I grew older, I began to realise that Billy's presence had nothing to do with the Springhill Farm end of his day but rather the busyness or otherwise of Johnny Barn, the auction mart just up Newchurch Road where he worked.

Billy wasn't a general farmer in the way Harry was, he had nothing to do with the hens, Diamond, rabbits and all the rest, he was more of a stockman. When he came with Glen, the farm dog, to bring the cows in, he carried a stout pole. He didn't hit the cows with it, but rather used it to guide them and he would twist their tails to keep them on track. It was very effective!

Billy was a cheery figure in those days, squirting milk at me from behind a cow, his blond curls bouncing as he laughed. He used a length of bale twine as a belt – I thought that was ever so funny! The brothers each had a special shiny bucket for the milk, we never put anything else into them, except water to swill them out when the milking session finished. Harry said they had to be kept special to keep the milk clean. Even if we ran short of buckets as the calves got bigger during the year, we never used those pails for their feed.

Close up, the cows themselves were big, smelly creatures. One or two of them were positively huge. Their tails whipped about in great swooshing arcs, their horny hoofs slid uncertainly on the wet cobbles of the yard or sank, squelching, into the slutch at the farm gate. Most of Harry's cows had horns, but three of them were what he called "pollys" - they had had their horns removed (pollarded). As time went on, more and more of his cows were pollys, he used to buy them from here and there, and horns were definitely going out of fashion.

I must have been six ("nearly seven") when I first went with Harry to bring the cows in. They were up in a sloping field which lay alongside the final section of the lane up to the council tip. I said it was going to be a long way to the top of the field to fetch them.

"Oh, no," he smiled at me. "They'll be down at the gate waiting. Come down a while before we want them in. We won't have to walk up to get them. You'll see. We might hear 'em first!"

I was puzzled. "Do they know what time it is?"

"Oh, aye. They know."

And they did. It seemed the cows not only knew the time, they got very annoyed if Harry was late. Sometimes they could be heard bellowing for him two fields away!

"Do you milk the cows every day?"

"Every day. Twice."

"Even on Sundays?"

"Yes. Cows don't know what day it is, do they?"

It was quite an education. Cows, it seemed, didn't know what day it was but they could tell the time!

Whichever field they were in, the cows were always waiting at the gate when Harry went for them. They would be restless and noisy, impatient to get home, crushing against the gate. It was quite rare for us to have to go and round one up. A few stragglers would take their time, but most of them were desperate to get into the shippen, pushing and shoving, slipping in their haste to get in. They would make quite a lot of noise too, annoyed with each other if they lost their place in this scramble.

Once at the shippen door, things quietened down a bit and the cows became more orderly. There seemed to be a pecking order – they certainly knew which stall was theirs, which surprises me to this day.

The shippen itself was a long, rectangular space with stalls for twelve cows. The stalls each had a metal pole with a big collar on a chain that slid up and down. The chains were just long enough for the cows to be able to lie down or stand, but not long enough for them to get their legs tangled up. It seemed to me that there was no need to tie the cows up; all they wanted was a bucket of feed and to relieve their bursting udders, but Harry said, no, they had to be tied up.

"Need 'em to stay put."

Actually, he was right. One winter morning, we opened up the shippen to find a young cow had slipped out of her collar and was just waiting on the cobbled stand by the milk churns.

"Collar's too big fert little un," he said. It was only one cow, once, and the animal was quite alright, but I suppose it could have slipped or even been kicked wandering about loose in there. I got the impression that Harry was cross with himself.

There was no heating in the shippen, but the cows generated their own warmth, there was always a cosy feel in there, even on the coldest days. Four bare light bulbs hung from the ceiling at intervals, and there was one cold water tap set into the wall alongside the milk churns. The cows had two buckets each, for food and water, but these were not like normal buckets or the pails used for the milk. These were big, squat, round metal buckets with no shaping to them at all. Their large diameter meant that even the biggest cow could get its head safely in and out and right to the bottom without getting stuck. They were also ancient. Goodness knows when they had been new – were they ever new? They had been bashed and kicked and scraped about forever. Great dents made some unstable and a few had been repaired so many times there wasn't much of the original bucket left at all. They had handles that rattled and made quite a racket as the cows pushed them about in the stalls. I didn't ever move the water buckets, they were far too heavy, but when I had got to about ten ("nearly eleven"), Harry used to let me help measuring the feed.

The feed for the cows was a combination of cattle cake and sugar beet which we mixed together. It was quite tasty if I got a bit peckish! It was kept in a little storeroom across from the shippen in big barrels with tight-fitting lids. I must have been about nine before I could even get the lids off! We had an old metal scoop for measuring and I thought how handy it was that the scoop had a special place to put your thumb – a bit like an artist's palette. *(It wasn't until 2019, watching an antiques programme featuring old farming implements that I realised that this "thumb hold" was actually where a wooden handle had been torn off.)*

I didn't like that storeroom. It was very still and very quiet in there. As well as all the animal feed, Harry kept rabbits in cages in that room. There was one huge white rabbit with red and pink eyes, which he said was a New Zealand rabbit and then three or four smaller black Dutch rabbits. Why Harry kept those rabbits is beyond me. He did once kill and skin one when I was there, but he wasn't really a rabbit farmer!

Back to the cows . . . it was always back to the cows really. Once milked and fed, they were each given an armful of hay if they were staying in for the night. Some of them would really settle in, I remember one of the big pollys used to lie down almost immediately, thoroughly content, her huge brown body filling the stall and she would chew the cud and dream polly dreams while buckets rattled and chains sawed up and down the poles all around her.

The milk was poured from the special pails through a fine mesh into the big milk churns which were collected from a stand at the side of Edge Lane every morning by a lorry from the Milk Marketing Board in Accrington. The churns made a special metallic clanging noise when they were empty, but didn't make a sound when they were rolled down the yard full of milk.

"Empty vessels make most noise," I told Harry. "We learned that at school."

"You learn a lot at that school," he said.

(That churn stand and a couple of outside toilets have been demolished. It's a parking space now!)

There was so much to learn about cows. Harry told me about different breeds – Ayrshire, long horn, short horn, Friesian, Hereford, Aberdeen Angus . . . he didn't have all these types, but we discussed them solemnly.

I suggested we could have a Highland cow, but he just laughed at that!

"What about Jersey cows?" I asked him, thinking of cows in storybooks. "Do you ever have them?"

He shook his head. "Never had 'em. Our grazin' aint good enough."

This brought a new dimension. Now we were talking about the quality of grass! I don't think that at seven years old, I had previously given much thought to the topic. I began studying fields in earnest, and it was interesting how many different sorts of grass I came across even in that restricted area. But, no, the grass at Springhill Farm wouldn't pass muster for a Jersey cow and we weren't about to get one! We never did either.

(In 1981, I persuaded a bemused couple of friends to come with me to an agricultural show in Adelaide, South Australia. My friends went off to the beer tent, but I spent quite some time looking at the Charolais cattle. I hadn't come across them before. We certainly didn't have them at Springhill Farm.)

Then there were milk yields to consider. The huge Friesian which always had the third stall in from the door produced the most milk by far. Although I don't think we ever measured the actual milk, you could tell it produced the most because it took much longer to milk than the others. So how long does it take to milk a cow by hand?

"Depends," said Harry.

As I learnt more and more at school about weights and measures, I would ferry vital pieces of information to the farm and Harry and I would chew them over.

Sometimes I think I must have driven him up the wall with my endless questions, but, you know, I think, looking back, that he enjoyed it. Gallons and pints, quarts and gills, we multiplied and divided til none of it made sense! And all the time, Harry worked steadily along his line of cows, filling the pails and churns with endless milk.

(In 2020, I came across a book in Rawtenstall Library called "How To Measure a Cow" by Margaret Forster. Of course, I borrowed it, but it wasn't really about cattle. I was most disappointed!)

Four

Newchurch School

I can be absolutely sure when I was in Mrs Halliwell's class at Newchurch School. When we returned to her classroom after the Christmas holidays, she had chalked up 1 9 6 0 in huge numbers on her blackboard. This, she told us, was the start of a new year, a new decade. She seemed to think this was very important. It must have been, because, temporarily, these numbers replaced Mrs Halliwell's usual chalk drawings of Janet and John.

Mrs Halliwell's class comes to me in snatches. We had painting sessions wearing smeared smocks with jam jars of mud-coloured water at little wooden easels, we started to learn about fractions, there were reading sessions every day, lining up by her desk to read to her. Lots of songs – Mrs Halliwell thumped the piano – and stories. We got as far as mastering the four times table. But it's funny how memory works, I can never remember writing, or learning to write. We had wooden rulers too and Mrs Halliwell wasn't above using one to rap some naughty boy across the knuckles on occasion.

But those times were very few. Mostly the classroom was a busy, jolly place; Mrs H was built like Hattie Jacques, a bustling, matronly figure with a bottle blonde perm, and she certainly got the most out of her six-year-old charges.

(I met Mrs Halliwell when she retired with her husband to St Annes. I was working as a reporter on the weekly newspaper there, and she invited me to her home. I was seventeen. The trouble was, of course, that I could only relate to her as a six-year-old child; I found having an adult conversation with her quite difficult. Heaven help me with the Spence family!)

Come September and a new pair of Start Rite shoes, I moved up a year – quite literally. Miss Bainbridge's class was not only upstairs, it was on the school stage! I liked Miss Bainbridge, she had her hair on top of her head, fastened with a large, ceramic slide. (Never seen the like!) We battled on with our tables, chanting every morning – I think we got as far as the eight times table that year. And the spellings! To this day, there are some words I spell out in my head the way Miss Bainbridge taught us; she broke the letters into chunks to make it easier. No phonics with this, just the simple naming of letters. So "peo … ple". Or "bec . . . ause". The whole class would chant it out as she tapped the letters on the blackboard. Of course, the chanting of tables and spellings wouldn't get houseroom nowadays, but funnily enough, it seemed to work.

I realise now that Miss Bainbridge must have been quite young. She didn't stay long at the school and I heard that she went to New Zealand – which I was quite certain was wrong. It was outrageous; New Zealand was on the other side of the world! Obviously, nobody would go and live so far away!

It was a happy life at Newchurch school. With its uncomplicated, predictable rhythms of the year, there was a solid, steady reliability which I loved then and treasure now. Harvest festival, conkers, nativity play, spring chicks, Easter egg painting, sports day . . . They all came round, accompanied by suitable hymns and poetry. Actually, some of those hymns were just dire – at one time I thought if I had to sing "We plough the fields and scatter" just once more, I would scream right there and then! On the other hand, we learned "Jerusalem", which seemed very daring and never appeared in our church services.

And so I made my way through the school, arriving at the 12 times table and Mr Kennedy's top class more or less simultaneously in September, 1963.

Mr Kennedy had what Mrs Spence would call "big ideas". He did too, but while Mrs Spence was forever frowning on big ideas, Mr Kennedy let rip. He taught us about decimals, he let us choose our own reading books, he had us listen to singing programmes on the radio, he ran a little biscuit shop at playtime. We did scientific experiments with mirrors and magnets, and he had a large, barely portable tape recorder with two big spools of tape.

But he had something else as well, something which was to influence me more than either he or I could ever have dreamed. Mr Kennedy was a big cricket fan. I had no interest in cricket and may well never have taken any notice, except that in order to help the boys (and it was unashamedly the boys in those days) follow that year's MCC tour of Australia, he pinned up a huge map of Australia on the wall. Over the days and weeks, Mr Kennedy would place little markers on the map to show where the team was now playing and he had a notebook where he had the various scores written down to discuss with the children who were interested. Some of them were indeed very interested, but I wasn't one of them. What I was interested in was the map itself; just imagine going there!

At that time, in the early 1960s, there were various programmes for children on the radio. "Listen With Mother" was probably the most famous, aimed at pre-school children who were still at home with their mothers, but there was also the BBC Radio Schools Service. Amongst the service's output was "Singing Together" presented by the ever-enthusiastic William Appleby.

Mr Kennedy acquired the little booklets of words, illustrated with line drawings, which accompanied the weekly programme and on Monday mornings Mr Appleby taught us traditional, popular songs. Every year, on The Last Night of the Proms, I send silent thanks to Mr Appleby – I can sing Hearts of Oak and Rule, Britannia! with the best of them! And all thanks to that little 30-minute programme.

I have included some of the songs and poetry I learned at Newchurch School here. I sometimes reflect how the songs, the poems, the chanting of spellings and tables actually helped the school as a whole by giving us all the same work and keeping us all at the same pace, helping all of us in our different ways to help each other. For me personally, I have ended up with a little treasure chest of sayings and songs, snatches of this and that, which lead my astonished sons to ask, "How do you know all this stuff?"

Songs.

British Grenadiers

Some talk of Alexander and some of Hercules,
Of Hector and Lysander and such great names as these,
But of all the world's great heroes,
There's none that can compare,
With a tarra, rara, rara, ra, to the
British Grenadiers.

(This is brilliant for marching home from school down Newchurch Road. You should try it some time!)

Hearts of Oak

Come cheer up me lads, 'tis to glory we steer,
To add something more to this wonderful year,
To honour we call them, as true men not slaves,
For who are so free as the sons of the waves?
Hearts of oak are our ships,
Jolly tars are our men,
We always are ready,
Steady, boys, steady.
We'll fight and we'll conquer
Again and again.

Donkey Riding

Were you ever in Quebec, stowing timbers on the
deck,
Where there's a king with a golden crown,
Riding on a donkey.
Hey ho, away we go,
Donkey riding, donkey riding,
Hey ho, away we go,
Riding on a donkey.

*(Arriving in Quebec in 1979, I sang this little song to
my bemused boyfriend! The trouble with this one is
that it is very catchy, and won't leave me alone for
days.)*

Rule, Britannia!

When Britain first at heaven's command…
Arose from out the azure main,
Arose, arose, arose from out the azure main.
This was the charter, the charter of the land,
And guardian angels shall command:
Rule, Britannia!
Britannia rules the waves,
Britons, never, never, never shall be slaves.

*(This never made any sense. I mean "as your main"
what? I smile about that every year when I watch
The Last Night of the Proms! I had a secondary
school teacher who berated the choir over a Latin*

carol we were learning. "You can't sing it unless you understand it," he said. Oh, yes, you can!)

The Minstrel Boy

The minstrel boy to the war is gone,
In the ranks of death you'll find him.
His father's sword he has girded on
And his wild harp slung behind him.

(This has a lovely melody and is regularly played on Remembrance Sunday at the Cenotaph in London. Not an obvious one for children to sing, but I always find it quite moving.)

We also learnt some words to **Schubert's Trout quintet**!

A clear and sparkling brooklet flowed on its merry way,
And in the crystal waters, a trout flashed by in play.
I stood awhile and rested and watched with pure delight,
The fish dart like an arrow in waters clear and bright.
The fish dart like an arrow in waters clear and bright.

(Never let it be said that Mr Kennedy didn't have aspirations for us. Nonetheless, I have always thought this was a particularly ambitious choice for a village school – but why not?)

These are not all the songs I can remember from those singing sessions. Others include The Raggle Taggle Gypsies ("Oh, what care I for a goose feather bed?" What indeed!), What Shall We Do With the Drunken Sailor and Au Te De Naus (which we sang in English except for the Welsh chorus.)

Poems.

Silver by Walter de la Mare.

Slowly, silently, now the moon
Walks the night in her silver shoon;
This way and that, she peers and sees
Silver fruit upon silver trees;
One by one the casements catch
Her beams beneath the silvery thatch;
Crouched in his kennel, like a log,
With paws of silver sleeps the dog;
From their shadowy cote the white breasts peep
Of doves in silver feathered sleep
A harvest mouse goes scampering by,
With silver claws, and silver eye;
And moveless fish in the water gleam,
By silver reeds in a silver stream.

(I used to think of Glen crouched in his kennel when we were learning this, but a less poetic sort of creature I can hardly imagine!)

Sea Fever by John Masefield.
(I can only remember the first two lines!)

I must go down to the seas again, to the lonely sea
and the sky,
And all I ask is a tall ship and a star to steer her by.

Cargoes by John Masefield.

Quinquireme of Nineveh from distant Ophir,
Rowing home to haven in sunny Palestine,
With a cargo of ivory,
And apes and peacocks,
Sandalwood, cedar wood and sweet white wine.

Stately Spanish galleon coming from the Isthmus,
Dipping through the Tropics by the palm- green
shores,
With a cargo of diamonds,
Emeralds, amethysts,
Topazes and cinnamon and gold moidores.

Dirty British coaster with a salt-caked smoke stack,
Butting through the Channel in the mad March days,
With a cargo of Tyne coal,
Road-rails, pig-lead,
Firewood, iron-ware and cheap tin trays.

*(I love this one. Mind you, it's amazing that any of us
got past the first word! On a sailing boat off
Indonesia in 1990, I pictured myself "dipping
through the tropics by the palm green shores", but it*

is the final verse which really has a good rhythm and
we used to clatter it out on the tops of our desks.
Great fun!)

From Love's Labour's Lost
(Act V, scene ii)
William Shakespeare

When icicles hang by the wall,
And Dick the shepherd blows his nail,
And Tom bears logs into the hall,
And milk comes frozen home in pail,
When blood is nipped and ways be foul,
Then nightly sings the staring owl,
Tu-whit
Tu-who! A merry note
While greasy Joan doth keel the pot.

(I only know the first verse of this poem.
*   Harry told me he had learned it at school too; it*
was Shakespeare.
*   "It's not!" I scoffed, confident at ten years old.*
"It's just a poem."
*   "Aye, it is, it's Shakespeare," he said. But of*
course, I was having none of it. As if Harry would
know Shakespeare – although of course I didn't say
that. Even at ten, I had some tact!
*   At Christmas in 2017, I was given a poetry*
anthology of the poem-a-day variety. I like this sort of
thing – just a little snippet of something on a daily
basis. But on January 20, 2018, I just about fell out of
my chair. There it was, "When icicles hang by the

39

wall" by William Shakespeare. So, fifty odd years later, I had to admit Harry was right! I should have known . . .)

Five

Springhill Farm

If you had wanted to visit Springhill Farm, you would arrive in Higher Cloughfold, go up Edge Lane for about 80 yards and then turn left into a narrow cobbled lane. This led past a short row of cottages and then the lane stopped and you would be at the farm gate.

For me, however, it was a bit different. All I had to do was leave the back kitchen door of Springhill, nip up a short path, round the cottage gardens and arrive at the farm gate. It would take me, maybe a minute.

In reality, chances were that you would be in the gateway rather than at the gate. A traditional, wooden five-barred gate, it was rarely closed. It occurs to me now that Harry may well have shut it when he left for the night and opened it first thing in the morning, but as far as I was concerned, it was always open. Even on Wednesdays, when we took Diamond and the cart to Rawtenstall for the provin, we didn't close the gate. ('Provin' was the word we used for the animal feed. I think it must have been a short form of 'provisions'.)

It is quite difficult to accurately describe the farm, because most of it was higgledy piggledy, but beyond the gateway, the cobbled yard opened out, with a series of buildings stretching up on the left and a large Dutch barn at the top. On the right, actually in the yard was a well built into the wall of a small field accessed by another wooden five-barred gate. This gate was usually shut, although the only livestock in that field – known as the Croft – were the hens, bantams, ducks and geese, which were all quite capable of squeezing through or under the gate.

There were various buildings in use, semi-use or derelict. Some were solid, stone-built structures with traditional slate roofing, others had started off life like that but had acquired wooden repairs or metal doors. Two or three of the smaller buildings had been whitewashed years before; some roofing had been patched up with tarpaulin. Up by the side of the Dutch barn was the wide metal barred gate to the main field and it was through this gateway that the cows came in, twice a day, for milking.

By the time I arrived on the scene, it was all a bit ramshackle, but of course I didn't see it like that then. In some ways it actually was a child's idea of a farm. We are not in Enid Blyton territory here – no sunlit orchards and red-tiled roofs, not even a friendly pony or an obedient sheepdog. But it was mixed farming – no modern lines of black and white cows with ear tags, no metal cages holding hundreds of miserable chickens, no huge rolls of hay in ghastly black plastic. This was about cows with horns, pitch forks, hay-making complete with horse-drawn dray, egg collecting and endless hours of sweeping the yard. It can't have made economic sense, but for a six-year-old it was just the job.

To describe the Croft as a small field gives the wrong impression. It was more like a muddy, stony area with some very large trees and a bit of grass on the far side. In the far wall was a wide wooden gate which led out onto Conway Road. That gate was seldom used except when we were hay-making and Diamond would bring the dray from the top field, down Conway Road and then into the Croft using that upper gate. The bottom gate into the yard was directly opposite.

The henhouse and a duck pond were the only features of the Croft so poultry had the run of it. And what a mess they made! The ground was just a huge slippery mess and my wellies hadn't got particularly good grips so I was constantly trying not to fall over. And if I wasn't steadying myself in this sludgy wasteland, I was trying not to stumble over the enormous tree roots that spread about everywhere. Not my favourite part of the farm!

The pond was particularly nasty – I couldn't imagine any self-respecting duck would want to swim in its dark, murky water. It had layers of green floating scum and stone sides plastered with slime. The ducks, maybe nine or ten of them, would cluster about a foot from the edge and chatter among themselves, probably grumbling about the state of the housekeeping service! I am always surprised that Harry didn't clean out that pond, but in my time there, he never did. In fact he rarely paid it any attention at all. There was a certain amount of excitement when he acquired three Muscovy ducks (goodness knows why or even where from), but other than that the ducks were just left to get on with life. They were rounded up and ushered into a little stone hut each evening, shut in behind a wooden door that came down on runners like a guillotine. The three geese were in there too, but I made a point of having nothing to do with the geese. In fact, I avoided them like the plague.

Well, to be more accurate, I avoided the big, white goose. That goose could strike terror into the hardiest – even Mrs Spence didn't like it, although she probably wasn't afraid of it. I can see her now, hanging out her washing, snapping a towel at it to leave her alone. It was quite a big bird too. It hissed like mad and ran towards me, flapping its wings and honking. To make matters worse, it was pretty much useless as far as I could tell. Great noisy thing!

But if the ducks couldn't get the staff, the hens certainly could! They had a very comfortable life.

The hen house was a place of mystery. It stood more or less in the middle of the Croft, a dark brown wooden shed lifted above the hard mud on stacks of stubby stones. From the outside, it appeared as an elevated hut, inside it became a sort of Tardis for chickens. Its gloomy interior stretched back from the door, with tiers of nesting boxes, feathers, dust and noise. There were several rails for roosting and a small space right down on the floor where the bantams could get some peace away from the bigger, bossy hens.

The chickens squabbled endlessly, clucking and fussing in their nests of hay, scratching and circling to make themselves that little extra bit more comfortable. The nesting boxes themselves were old wooden pop bottle crates.

During the day, the hen house door stood open and its occupants spilled out onto the compact mud. Gradually, having investigated the galvanised chicken feeders for breakfast, the hens would cluck and peck their way down under the gate into the cobbled yard. The chickens kept up an almost constant chatter, squawking with indignation if they had to give way to Diamond or if Billy tried to kick them out of the way.

I tried many times to count the chickens, but it was a losing battle.

"How many hens have you got, Harry?"

"A fair few. Have you not got them counted yet?" He laughed – it was impossible.

"I have counted the bantams! You've got nine," I told him, proud of myself. "And ten ducks and three geese."

"Sounds about right. You just need to get cracking with them hens!"

About tea time, just before we went to get the cows in for the evening milking, the hens would be shut away for the night. Most would have already made their way into the hen house, but there were always some which needed rounding up. I would run around the top of the Croft, herding the chickens home, while Harry sent the few left in the yard or the Upper Croft scurrying in before the door was closed. He always closed the door very tightly, checking the bolts and wedging a brick between the top step and the door so that it couldn't possibly come open accidentally.

"Don't want them getting out," he said. "Or anything getting in neither."

"You mean robbers?" I was wide-eyed.

"Might be a fox about," he said darkly. "Can't be too careful with foxes."

Persuading the ducks to go into their little stone hut at night was much easier. Mostly they just waddled home when the hen round-up began. The geese, noisy, pointless birds in my opinion, followed them in and the door came down on its runners. The Croft was shut down for the night.

As I grew older, the routine of it all seemed deadening.

"You do this every day, Harry! Every day of your life!"

"Oh aye, every day," he said.

Eggs were collected each morning. We used the grain scoop to carry them and, as I grew older, Harry let me take them down to Mrs Spence at the house. I felt the enormity of this responsibility quite keenly. The eggs weren't heavy, but they rolled around in the metal scoop, bumping into each other and threatening to crack with every step. I would hold the scoop with both hands and walk slowly down the cobbles.

Mrs Spence had large cardboard egg trays waiting for the next batch. When the trays were full, she stored them in a little cellar which she entered through a trapdoor at the back of the living room. I never went into that cellar. It wasn't a big, roomy place like the cellar at Springhill. More of a cave with shelves. If Mrs Spence was in a good mood, she would give me a bantam egg. "Here's one for your tea," she'd say. "Don't break it."

"We could have the egg trays up here at the farm," I said to Harry one day as he filled the scoop with a fresh collection. "We could fill them here instead of at the house."

"We could," he said. But we didn't.

"You know, there are thirty-six eggs in each of those trays," I told him. "Six rows of six. Six sixes are thirty-six."

"Aye. Three dozen. That's right," he said.

"Twelve in a dozen," I said solemnly. "Three times twelve is thirty-six. So it's just the same!"

"Proper little mathematician, aren't you?" he grinned.

"Oh no. It's just tables. We do them every day at school."

Six

A Farmer's Wife

Mrs Spence had that wonderful north country combination of being able to strike terror and dispense kindness in equal measure. In the same moment, I could be scared stiff and reassured.

Harry (and I suppose Billy and Betty) called her Mother. Everyone else called her Mrs Spence. It was years before it occurred to me that she might have a Christian name!

In the years I knew her, Mrs Spence was in her early seventies, a thin, wiry woman with a grey curly perm, which was the fashion for women of her age then. (I have to say that "fashion" isn't a word which springs readily to mind when considering Mrs Spence.) She had standards though. She wore thick stockings and shoes – never slippers – even in the house, and over her skirt and cardigan she would wear a full-length apron – but not a housecoat.

Once a week, she donkey-stoned the three stone steps up to the house door. It was actually the back door, but it was the only one ever used. The front door, which was never used, was off the parlour and nobody ever used that either. I once peeped round the long velveteen curtain which hid the parlour door and had a glimpse of that room. I remember it being quite

48

dark with huge furniture. This was a typical set-up for the time; there was a best room at the front of the house but the family essentially lived in the main back room, which in this case was a kitchen, dining room and sitting room all in one.

I wasn't exactly frightened of Mrs Spence, just forever wary, I could never be sure what sort of reception awaited me. I would hand her the scoop full of eggs and she'd say things like "pass them here, just take your time and be quick about it!"

She didn't like "our 'arry" being mithered and instructed that I was not to get under his feet. On summer afternoons, I would slip round to the house after my lunch to see if Harry was ready to go up the yard after his dinner. Quite often he would be asleep at the table. Mrs Spence, ever alert, would point silently at the one other dining chair. This was my cue. If I spoke, she would send me home, no question. If I sat quiet, I would be allowed to wait.

After a few minutes, Harry would rouse himself. He would clean his teeth at the kitchen sink with toothpaste from a little round tin, and then we'd be off. Time to sweep the yard. That cobbled yard was swept every day and the monotony of it eventually drove me away. By the time I was nine, I didn't go to the farm much in the afternoons – it was better to go later when the cows were coming in.

Mrs Spence had a very predictable routine as well. She must have washed laundry every day. Of course, she was doing all the laundry for four adults by hand – takes some doing! Every morning, she climbed the stone steps across from the house and hung the day's washing out on a line. It was a funny patch of ground up there – nobody seemed to look after it, but it never got overgrown. The geese sometimes managed to get through from the Croft, I could never work out how they did that, but Mrs Spence didn't want their company and would shoo them away sharpish.

The laundry dominated domestic life. Once back inside the house, Mrs Spence would arrange huge woollen socks on a wooden clotheshorse placed in front of the coal fire.

(In 2019, I spoke to John Mansergh at the corn merchants in Rawtenstall. I asked him if he had known Mrs Spence.

Oh yes, he chuckled, he knew her.

"She was a bit fierce," I said.

"Well, she was a farmer's wife. They were expected to be fierce!" he said.

And I think that's just about it, but I am not about to say she was really as soft as butter!)

The other person at the farmhouse was Betty, Harry and Billy's younger sister. I only saw Betty if I went round to the house in an evening – which was not very often – because she worked in one of the mills in Rawtenstall and so was not about during the day. Occasionally I would see her coming home in her flat brown shoes and long gaberdine raincoat. She had a brown leather bag too. It was like a uniform.

Offhand, I couldn't remember seeing Betty up the yard, but it wasn't until years later that Harry told me that she never, ever, set foot on the farm.

"Never come up," he said. "Even at hay-making. Mother would come and help muck out while we got the hay in, but Betty wouldn't. She had nowt to do wi' it."

Betty was a friend of my aunt Dorothy, my mother's youngest sister, who still lived at Springhill with my grandparents. The two of them would watch Coronation Street together in the farmhouse - who could have imagined the programme would last all these years! There was a lot of knitting going on as well. Betty was particularly quick and she tucked one needle right under her arm to hold it still while the other flashed back and forth. There was a little counter stuck on the end of one needle to tot up the number of rows she managed. Mrs Spence didn't knit, but she did watch Coronation Street and admonished us all about the perils of chilblains.

Sometimes, you don't realise what you're looking at. I was quite excited one Saturday morning to find Betty mixing something in a bowl with a wooden spoon. She told me she was making a cake.

I looked at her, puzzled. This wasn't how a cake was made in our house.

She smiled at me. "Does your Mummy have a mixer?" she said.

Yes, she did. And she had a washing machine too. And we had drying rods over the Aga. We had enough chairs for us all to sit at the table together. We had a bathroom sink to clean our teeth and the toilet was inside the house. What I was watching, day after day, was poverty in action.

Next door to the Spence home lived Miss Holt and her brother. Miss Holt was a spry ancient woman, who remains the only person I have known to wear clogs in their daily life; I doubt she owned a pair of ordinary shoes. Her clogs were not the brass-nailed, highly-polished footwear favoured by today's Morris dancers and town criers. These were poor, ill-fitting things. They were made of dull, black leather with straps across the top of Miss Holt's bony feet. You could see the gaps down the sides where they didn't fit her properly and must have rubbed terribly. It makes my feet sore just to think about them. As Miss Holt didn't have a carpet, or even a rug that I could see from the door, she clattered across the stone floor, dressed always in black and was altogether a child's idea of a witch.

What Miss Holt did have though, which I have always loved, was a deep, Rossendale voice. It is a timbre like no other and very few women have it, but she did. One of my great aunts, who lived in Waterfoot, had it too. I hear it very occasionally to this day, and I always end up thinking of Miss Holt!

Where Miss Holt was surprisingly energetic, her brother rarely moved. He wore a black suit, complete with jacket at all times, and sat at the end of the range. This was a huge, traditional thing which took up the whole of the side wall of their kitchen-living room. As I never got any further than the doorstep of that house, I am not sure if Miss Holt's brother wore clogs as well, but he probably did.

Next along were Mr and Mrs Cunliffe. Mrs Cunliffe was small and asthmatic. She had a pump to help her breathe and to use it she had to fit a black rubber mask over her face. Mr Cunliffe was also short, but he was quite portly and he played bowls. I would see him at the bus stop sometimes with his special bowls bag. I got to know Mr and Mrs Cunliffe quite well because their granddaughter, June, would come and spend part of her summer holidays with them and she was my age. Mrs Cunliffe used to dry melon seeds on her windowsill so that June and I could make little bracelets, and she had sticky strips of paper hanging from the ceiling to catch flies.

There was one other cottage in that row, but I have no idea who lived there. The door was never open.

Finally, there was Mrs Murgatroyd's bungalow. You won't find it there now – it seems to have developed into a two-story house! Mrs Murgatroyd had a beautiful garden full of geraniums. She knew my Granny quite well and once tried to interest me in an old wooden doll's cradle she had in the living room. I don't think she got quite the response she was hoping for! These dolls' cradles pop up on antiques programmes sometimes – I find myself straight back at Mrs Murgatroyd's.

Seven

Horse and Hound

The carthorse, Diamond, was one of only two animals on the farm which had a name. She was a big, dapple grey mare – probably not quite as huge as she is in my memory – and she had a stable all to herself down by the main farm gate, next to the wash-house.

It was quite a big room, with two large stalls and a wooden wall ladder which reached right up into the hay loft. The ladder was really a very long plank with holes cut into it for feet and hands. I only ever climbed it once, it was riddled with worm. I'm not sure I ever saw Harry climb it, but come hay-making, when the yard came alive with men helping with the harvest, Billy would nip straight up that ladder and think nothing of it.

The stable floor was the ubiquitous cobbles and Diamond's shoes scraped back and forth; she rarely lay down, but would stand docile, with her eyes half closed and one of her hind legs tilted so that just the tip of her hoof remained on the ground. It's a common enough stance for a horse, but whenever I see a horse standing like that, I am straight back in that stable, in the dim light, watching Diamond with my six-year-old eyes.

At the front of her stall – she always had the right hand one – was an old-fashioned manger, which Harry would tip her feed into. She would also have a big bucket of water and a couple of armfuls of hay stuck up in a hay rack above her head. And she had a salt lick. I was fascinated with this, a big, pink solid block of salt with a hole drilled right through so it could be fastened to the side of the stall. To this day, I can't imagine why it was pink, or even how it got that colour. The cows had a salt lick too, but they had to share and it hung on the field gate which led to the lane going up to the tip.

Diamond's tack was kept in the stable with her. The bridle, patched and repatched with tape to hold the blinkers in place hung on a nail by the door. The big collar, with stuffing poking out of the seams, took up another two nails. The rest of the harness for pulling the carts – straps, chains, buckles – lay on a rough wooden shelf by the bridle. There was a rope halter of sorts, but Harry rarely used it. He sometimes stuffed it in his pocket, but usually he would just call her in from the field and she would come.

"Don't need to catch it. It comes any road."

And, I suppose, that was about the size of it, Diamond did come towards him any road.

When Diamond was needed, we would venture into the field, Harry holding a black rubber bucket with some calves' nuts in the bottom. A few paces in, he would bang on the side of the bucket. It was an odd sound, a sort of dullness in the thick rubber, but evidently it was a sound that carried. Within moments of this noise starting, Diamond, sometimes right across the field, would lift her head and gaze at us.

She considered for a few moments and then began her customary steady walk towards us, lumbering along, no hurry, but purposeful. Sometimes, a few nosey young bullocks would try to get in on the act, jostling each other to reach the bucket, but something about Diamond would stop them in their tracks. As she helped herself to the nuts, Harry would sling the halter rope or a length of bale string round her neck and lead her into the yard.

She was only ever kept in those two places – the stable or the yard field. Throughout the year, the cows moved from field to field, even up onto the moor, but Diamond was always close to home.

Harry was fond of that mare; I think he appreciated the effort she put in. Often, when he was bringing her out from between the cart shafts after a day's work, he would give her three or four mint Imperials which he had in his pocket. She liked them! I could hear her crunching them, her great head nodding up and down. And if I was lucky, Harry would give me a sweet too!

One spring, when the snow had disappeared and there was finally a little bit of sun, Harry decided to let Diamond out into the field for the day.

"It'll like that," he said. "Watch."

We thumped up the cobbles to the field gate, slow at first, but suddenly Diamond picked up pace with her ears pricked. She snorted and shook her head – this was serious action in carthorse terms!

Harry opened the gate and let her go. Diamond all but trotted out and then suddenly, she lay on the ground and started rolling from side to side, her great hooves thrashing through the air.

"Oh!" I remember gasping at the sight. "Did you know she would do that?"

"Thought it might. Bin inside a long time o'r winter."

"Are we going to let the cows out now – just for the day, I mean?"

"Nah. Not yet. They'll have to wait a bit yet. Not warm enough."

He shut the gate and we turned back towards the shippen.

"Do you think it will snow some more before we can let the cows out?" I asked him.

"Shouldn't think so, just needs to warm up a bit."

A thought struck me.

"You know how we get the cows in for the winter before the snow comes and don't let them out til it's over? It means that cows never see snow, they might get scared if they saw their fields all white - they don't know what snow is!"

"Come again?"

I went over my theory with him.

He nodded. "That'll be right enough. I never thought of that."

The other animal on the farm with a name was Glen, the dog. This dog was a horror and I hated him from first to last! He was kept in a small shed up near the field gate on a long length of thick chain. A muddy brown colour, he barked at just about everything and jumped up and down, the chain clanking on the small strip of concrete outside the shed-kennel. The hens squawked at him furiously – but they kept their distance! I don't think Harry liked him much either – but Billy did. Billy would let Glen off the chain and bring him up to the moor gate when we were bringing the cows in at teatime. Horrible mutt, he ran around annoying the cows; I saw one of them kick him once. Thankfully, even when running about like that, he was never interested in me.

Thinking about it now, I am a bit surprised Harry hadn't more time for Glen; maybe he just didn't want a dog loose on the yard and, as with all the animals, Glen wasn't a pet. He was a guard dog of sorts, I suppose, certainly nobody got up that yard unnoticed. The racket that dog made with his barking and growling and his rattling chain!

Long after my time there, Diamond died at the farm. The knacker was sent for and he duly arrived. Apparently he took one look and declared that Diamond was so big, he couldn't fit the body in his vehicle and so he would have to cut her in half.

Mrs Spence was having none of it!

"Mother sent him off to get a bigger wagon," Harry told me. "She didn't want to see it cut up like that. She were hoppin' mad!"

I nodded. "Yes, awful," I said. What I didn't say was that Mrs Spence had almost certainly sent the man off with a flea in his ear because she didn't want Harry to see Diamond butchered like that. Good for her!

Eight

Newchurch Church

Next door to the school, slightly higher up the hill was St Nicholas Church, where we attended weekly as a family and held our weddings, christenings, funerals and memorial services as appropriate. We didn't call it St Nicholas though, it was always "Newchurch church" to us.

The church dates to Tudor times, but for the most part its long, impressive history was lost on me as a child. I did go up its tower one May morning, but the real stand-out memory for me is the autumn I went with my Granny to help decorate the church for harvest festival.

I was quite puzzled at the things we were taking with us for this outing: a tin bottle of Brasso, assorted dusters, the Hoover, wax polish, a stiff handbrush . . . None of the fruit, vegetables and flowers which I had expected.

We were busy! At first we were just a few helpers, some were sweeping round the pews, one lady was mopping the aisle, Granny herself got the vacuum cleaner going on the carpet by the altar, and I was put to work shining up the lectern with the Brasso and some dusters. The choir stalls and altar rail got a polish of wax too. Later, we were joined by others who brought boxes and crates of fruit, vegetables, flowers and little sheaves of hay. Some of the flowers were tied with ribbons, others were used to decorate the top of the pulpit. We had scissors and string and buckets, brushes, bins and sponges. Newchurch church was to look its best!

The lectern at St Nicholas is a brass column topped by an eagle spreading its wings to hold the open Bible. In 2017, attending a funeral service there, I saw it again, still gleaming at the foot of the chancel steps. And I smiled at the thought of all the Brasso that must have been used over all those years to keep it shining – never more so than in the autumn of 1963 when a girl of nine polished it for the harvest festival!

It wasn't far from Springhill to Newchurch. As the school and the church were next door to one another, it was the same walk whichever I was going to and this took me up Newchurch Road, across the top of Hareholme Lane and then through the housing estate along Staghills Road. Most of the children who went to Newchurch school lived on the Staghills estate, and so that was the way I walked home too, various friends peeling off as they reached their homes until I walked on by myself to Higher Cloughfold. The whole walk from school to Springhill took about twenty minutes. Or it would have done if we hadn't stopped off at the shop at the bottom of Top Barn Lane for a paper twist of kali or maybe some Mojos. (Kali is a sherbet dip, best sampled from a licked finger!) There was a chewing gum machine up on Newchurch Road near the top of Top Barn Lane and occasionally we went round by there as well. There were other diversions too, some children liked the little playground behind some houses, others balanced precariously along the garden walls. I didn't mind joining in with some of this – but it was never the main objective. Dawdling was all very well for others, but I needed to get home sharpish: Harry would be getting the cows in for milking and I didn't want to miss it!

I would skip along Newchurch Road, or sometimes pretend I was riding a pony. Johnny Barn, the auction mart, would be closed for the day by then and directly across the road from Johnny Barn, grey sheep would be grazing near the barbed wire fence. Tufts of wool stuck on the sharp spikes. It was years before I realised that the sheep were actually white – or at least cream-coloured – and the grey of their wool was pollution from the Rossendale mill chimneys. Now, those fields have been built on and a row of houses stands along the line of the barbed wire. Johnny Barn isn't there either. Nowadays we have Johnny Barn Close, a group of smart houses on the land once occupied by the auction mart's livestock sheds and open-air pens constructed of metal poles. Still, at least the name remains.

As walks home from school go, I reckon it was pretty good. By the time I'd passed Johnny Barn, it was just another few yards past Zion Baptist Church, across the end of Edge Lane and a quick skirt along the wall of Springhill to the main gate. Home.

And that's what it was like, day after day trotting home from school. It saddens me now to think that children don't experience that same freedom any more. You rarely see a child of that age out on their own, dreaming up little stories, trying to remember poems, wondering if a particular drain has been unblocked yet, kicking autumn leaves, lobbing the odd snowball. I was rarely met from school and I didn't expect to be; as children we spilled out of school and made our own ways home – it was all part of the day.

One year at the church there was great excitement. We were to put on a performance of Benjamin Britten's Noye's Fludde (Noah's Flood). The children of the Sunday School were to be all the animals going into the Ark. Some professional singers were brought in to take the main parts and the chorus was made up of members of the choir and various other singers seconded to bolster the ranks.

I'm not sure Newchurch church had ever seen the like. Anyway, we all duly rehearsed, which itself was pretty special, and then the great moment arrived. I was a panda. My Mum had made a panda's head for me to wear. It was a large black and white affair with mother-of-pearl buttons for eyes and the whole thing was then stitched onto a beret. Marvellous. Everyone had made a huge effort with these animal heads, and it must have been quite a sight as we all processed down the aisle.

The "animals" were ranged on the chancel steps behind the main singers and my place was right at one end. It was a good position; I found myself next to a man who was crouched on a small stool with a stick from which hung several teacups. The congregation couldn't see him, but I was fascinated. As Noah began to sing and the "rain" started, the teacups were gently rattled, swinging against each other to create the sound of raindrops. Then, as the storm built up and the music swelled, so the teacups bounced and bashed against each other. My first experience of sound effects!

Zion Baptist Church stood on the corner of Edge Lane, with a small graveyard at the front and some tatty outbuildings at the back. I had never been inside the building and didn't know anybody who had. One winter, they put on a pantomime and, rather to my surprise, a family who lived in the cottages along from the Red Lion, asked if I would like to go with them.

It was really good fun! I remember the panto, Aladdin, as a very colourful, rowdy experience with lots of gold drapery and a genie with a huge, jewelled turban. There were sweets and balloons and men with roaring voices. Children were jumping up and down and a piano thumped endlessly. There were loud bangs, lots of slapstick and boys whistling from the back of the hall. There must have been a story in there somewhere, but somehow that wasn't the point. I'd never seen anything like it!

There was all the usual panto stuff (oh yes there was!) – it was audience participation and then some. Fabulous.

But, in time, I would go to other pantomimes and shows and no doubt this first one in Higher Cloughfold would have seemed small fry and eventually forgotten if it hadn't been for one thing: in the midst of all this uproarious nonsense, we learned a song:

Alphabet Song (as sung at Aladdin, Zion Baptist Church)

A, you're adorable,
B, you're so beautiful,
C, you're a cutie full of charms,
D, you're a darling and
E, you're exciting and
F, you're a feather in my arms.
G, you're so good to me,
H, you're so heavenly,
I, you're the one I idolise,
J, you're like Jack and Jill,
K, you're so kissable,
L, you're the love light in my eyes.
M,N,O,P I could go on all day,
Q,R,S,T alphabetically speaking you are O K.
U make my life complete,
V means you're very sweet,
W,X,Y,Zee,
It's fun to wander through the alphabet with you,
And tell you what you mean to me!

The Alphabet Song must have been introduced very early in proceedings so that, once the audience had learned it, it could be used throughout the rest of the performance. Rowdiness hadn't yet set in and we dutifully sat there to learn "A, you're adorable, B, you're so beautiful," etc. I must have been the ideal child for this; I listened carefully, followed all the instructions and sang heartily. Once the audience was fully rehearsed, it only needed a pantomime character to leap out from the side of the stage and shout "A" and away we'd go!

I have never forgotten that song; I could sing it for you now if you like. And consequently, I shall never forget Aladdin at Zion Baptist Church.

Bonfire night was one of the highlights of the year. Initially, this consisted of a few sparklers on the lawn at Springhill, but when I was older I used to go to a bonfire at my friend Margaret's home. Margaret lived on Staghills estate, and her family's house backed onto an old lane near the football ground. This rough ground was perfect for the fire. It wasn't all that big as bonfires go, but it was just right for us and a few of Margaret's neighbours.

One year, my Mum suggested that as Margaret and her family had built the bonfire, we would supply the guy. We made him on the kitchen table at Springhill, dressed in big socks and an old pair of my Dad's pyjamas for trousers. He also had a pullover and a cap. Our guy caused quite a stir when we got him out of the car at Staghills!

Of course, you don't see spontaneous little bonfires like that anymore, but it was such good fun. There was homemade treacle toffee and we all wore mittens and waved our sparklers in the cold.

Newchurch church had a May Queen. Each year, an older girl from the Sunday school would be chosen as the Queen and several others selected as her attendants. Then at Whitsuntide there would be a parade, with banners and bands, the Mother's Union, the choir, the Sunday school and various other church organisations with the May Queen and her entourage as the focal point.

The parade would form up roughly outside the church and on up the hill into Newchurch village. At some signal, the parade would then process down Newchurch Road to Staghills Road, where it would turn left into the estate. Then, all the way through the estate back to the school. As parade routes go, it must have been an organiser's dream.

The banner for St Nicholas church is a huge, heavy thing. It is embroidered with the saint and has gold ropes with tassels. To carry it in the procession took several men with leather holsters for the poles and others for the guy ropes, and it must have been quite a responsibility. If the wind caught the banner it was literally like a ship's sail and I have seen men stagger right across the road to bring it back under control. (In 2012, I saw the great banner in the church porch. Some women who were there to arrange flowers told me that it no longer ever left the church, it's condition now too fragile for processions. I looked up at it leaning there against the wall, faded but still a great symbol of those long-ago days.)

The Mother's Union banner was smaller, more manageable, and didn't generate the same level of anxiety (in me at least)!

I was usually in the procession, but on at least one occasion I watched from the pavement by the entrance to Heightside on Newchurch Road.

The May Queen wore beautiful robes; often the outfit would be a full-length dress of satin or other rich material, and then a velvet cape with a train. She would have a tiara and sometimes elbow length gloves and flowers. The attendants would also have long dresses and flowers. To my eyes, it was lovely and so special.

In the winter of 1964, the axe fell. We were to leave Springhill. Not only leaving the house, but the life, the farm, everything, to go and live in County Durham. I was just eleven and desolation swept through me.

We left in December. I attended my last Sunday school class at the old Newchurch School and the young teacher sympathised with me.

I shall never forget what she said and how I have wished for the rest of my life that she hadn't said it: "It's such a shame you're leaving, you would have been next year's May Queen."

Nine

Rawtenstall – by Cart

Every Wednesday, after the morning milking finished and the cows were out in the fields for the day, we went down to Rawtenstall with Diamond and the cart to get the week's provin.

"Provin", the only word we ever used, meant all the animal feed. So, food not only for the cows, but also the calves, hens, ducks and Diamond. I can't remember us buying specifically for the rabbits or for Glen – I rather suspect that between them Harry and Mrs Spence got creative when it came to feeding them!

Harry was very careful; he always had me run home to check it was alright to go to Rawtenstall with him. As I grew older, I would know it was Wednesday so that when I arrived at the farm, I could tell him that I had permission already!

By the time the field gate closed behind the last of the cows, it would be mid-morning. Diamond would be fetched from her stable and kitted out with the harness for the cart. Some of those trappings were ancient. Sometimes, Harry would rub a little oil on the chain that fitted over a narrow leather saddle. This wasn't a saddle at all really, it was a sort of wide belt with a metal groove in it which fitted over Diamond's

68

back. The chain ran through the groove. Then there was a huge collar and the bridle, which should have been replaced years before and had blinkers held on with tape. I don't think the cart itself must have been all that heavy – Harry would haul it out into the yard himself and then back the mare between the shafts. Diamond knew the score; she backed up willingly, but sometimes if the angle was wrong, or her hooves slipped too much on the cobbles, Harry would have to lead her right out from the cart shafts and start the procedure all over again. Once she was settled between the shafts, the various chains and buckles would be fastened.

Finally ready, I would climb up on the cart wheel and hop over into the cart where I sat on the empty sacks which we were returning to the mill. Harry would nip into the wash house for a dark blue cotton jacket and his beret and away we went. Magic!

Funny how I remember that beret now. Such an inconsequential thing, really, but Harry never wore it on the farm and he never left the farm without putting it on. Even on very warm summer days, he would ditch the jacket, but not the beret.

The journey from Higher Cloughfold to Rawtenstall is not far, something over a mile, and I suppose it took us about twenty minutes. We were bound for Mansergh corn merchants in the centre of Rawtenstall. Harry walked at Diamond's head, holding her bridle all the way. I had a great view from up there in the cart, slowly passing the houses on Newchurch Road before turning left into Grange Road and making our way past Alder Grange secondary school. Of course, because I only did this trip during the holidays, the school was always shut up and deserted, but I always thought it looked quite inviting. From there, down into Bank Street, then a few side streets and there we were.

Harry usually knew what he wanted, but sometimes he would have a list in his back pocket. He kept a stubby pencil and some scraps of paper in the wash house at the farm for this purpose.

It was quite cool in the grain merchants' building. Diamond would pull the cart right inside, fitting snugly between two raised platforms which were at about the same height as the cart. This was quite handy for me – it meant I could just step over the side of the cart onto one of these platforms and wait while the sacks of provin were sorted out. We usually bought about the same amount, although not always the same thing. Sugar beet, cattle cake and calves' nuts (they were all for the cows) and then oats for Diamond and some food for the hens. The nuts were in thick paper bags with BOCM written in huge letters on the sides, but all the rest were in ordinary coarse brown hundredweight sacks. *(BOCM stood for British Oil and Cake Mills.)*

Harry and the men working there would speak to one another in a series of short, unintelligible bursts as the cart was steadily loaded. We never paid for any of it. Harry would speak to a man who sat behind a dusty glass window in the little office and, I assume, confirm what we had bought. Mrs Spence would pay later.

The journey back to Higher Cloughfold was a more comfortable ride; I would make a little hollow in one of the sacks of grain and enjoy the slow rocking motion of the cart as we made our way up the hill just in time for me to jump down and run off back to Springhill for lunch.

(In 2012, I was astonished to stumble across the corn merchants. So much of Rawtenstall centre had been altered and in the maze of a boarded-up shopping centre, I completely lost my bearings. As I emerged from the gloom of the mall, I came face to face with Mansergh's. Of all things, I recognised the door – it is a huge wooden door suspended from a rail like a tram track.

I approached the same old office window, briefly entertaining myself with the thought that it hadn't been cleaned since I was last there. I spoke to an elderly man who was busy reading a newspaper. What to say exactly?

"Excuse me."

"Yes, luv?" He didn't look up, which didn't help.

"Have you worked here a long time? I . . . I mean about fifty years."

Now he looked up.

"Near enough, I suppose."

"Did you know Harry Spence? He was a friend of mine."

"Oh, Harry," he chuckled. "Course I did!"

He peered at me through the glass. His eyes widened in astonishment as he looked at me and he didn't even try to keep the surprise out of his voice. "You? You were a friend of Harry's?")

Whilst the weekly trips to Rawtenstall for the provin were regular as clockwork, Harry once took me with him on a trip with Diamond and the cart to Waterfoot.

Instead of making our way down Newchurch Road towards Rawtenstall, we came down Peel Street between the Red Lion and Mrs Smith's corner shop as far as the top of Dobbin Lane. Then, instead of taking the very steep route down the rest of Peel Street, we took the slightly less demanding Dobbin Lane all the way down to Bacup Road. As far as I recall, that is the only time I have ever been on Dobbin Lane.

"Easier fert thorse," Harry told me. He didn't want Diamond sliding or slipping on Peel Street's steep drop to the bottom. Down on Bacup Road at Cloughfold, we turned left and headed towards Waterfoot.

Our destination turned out to be a long, low building on the outskirts of Waterfoot – a saw mill. Harry wanted sacks of sawdust and chippings to use as bedding for the calves. The saw mill was a haze of choking dust. Diamond didn't like it – and neither did I! Harry swung the cart right round so that the mare wasn't in the building itself but remained in the relatively fresh air. *(That building is still there, although it is no longer a saw mill. It's a shoe factory!)*

It was a funny little trip, we only ever did it that once, although I assume Harry did it often when I was at school. When we got back to the farm, Harry shook his beret to get rid of the sawdust and Diamond blew dust from her nose. All three of us drank lots of water!

Of course, there was plenty of water on the farm and a deep rectangular well on the yard itself, but one summer was so hot, we needed to do something extra. In the afternoons, we took Diamond and the cart right over to a stream somewhere just above Waingate. We had empty milk churns in the cart and filled them with water from a stream which at that point was gushing out of a huge concrete pipe. This was very hot, very heavy work; I didn't ride in the cart for this – Harry was conscious of Diamond having to pull the water churns quite some distance across bumpy tracks and even my eight-year-old weight came into his reckoning. We used the Croft's top gate and threaded our way along old tracks to the stream. Sometimes, if Billy had finished early at Johnny Barn, he would come and help with filling the churns and lifting them up into the cart. It must have been exhausting work in that heat.

But, needs must, and the cows needed the water; their bath-well in the main field was pretty much dried up and they got through gallons and gallons of water when they came in for the evening milking.

Ten

Of Walls and Drains

How many times these days do I walk alongside the old stone walls, or lean against them looking down into the river? The stones are infinitely variable: flat, jagged, mossy, slimy, sometimes gleaming in the rain. In summer sunshine they become warm, in winter they are solid blocks of cold.

It's not only walls that are stone, of course. Roads, barns, schools, endless rows of houses, mills . . . in short, just about everything. And the stones bear testament to the industrial past, blackened over decades by endless soot and smoke. Lots of buildings have been cleaned up now, and Springhill is one of them.

I remember the shock I got some time in the late 1990s when I saw the newly cleaned face of the house. It gives me a jolt even now, although I do think it looks smart. Springhill was the uniform black of every other property when I lived there. Nowadays, of course, many buildings have been cleaned so that the rows of houses give a patchwork effect lending another dimension to the use of stone.

But it's the stone walls that marked out every field that I remember most. You can still see them all over the Pennines and the north of England generally – it's particularly noticeable from a train. Mile upon mile of stone walls, marching over hillsides, delineating this boundary or that. I think of the man hours that must have been expended building them and the mind boggles. The carts, the horses, the sheer effort that must have been used to keep sheep or cattle from wandering.

Springhill farm was no different, the fields marked out by stone walls – and they had to be maintained. Like everything else, the job fell to Harry – I was his assistant. And for once, instead of being his shadow, or an observer, dry stone walling was something I could actually help with.

We used to march round the field walls fairly regularly, looking for damage or weak spots. You might have thought those walls were pretty solid, and indeed they were, but cattle rub up against them, pushing and shoving in their haste to get through a gate, or just wanting a good scratch. Cows, it goes without saying, are big heavy animals, easily able to dislodge stones as they saw back and forth to relieve an itch. Feisty bullocks, knocking each other about, can flip the flat top stones off a wall like frisbees.

So we would regularly come across walls that needed patching up or, even more exciting from my point of view, rebuilding.

The good part of this dry stone walling repair work was that all our components were already out there in the fields. We weren't building new walls; the stones used previously were all still there, scattered about in the grass or toppled over into ragged heaps.

As with all his work, Harry had a method for dealing with damaged walls. First, we had to sort the stones which had been dislodged. It was surprising how far from a wall some of those stones would travel; I suppose they would get kicked by the cows or maybe the smaller ones would fly out from the wall as a section tumbled. While Harry made a pile of the larger, flatter stones, my job was to run about collecting up all the small, sometimes very small, scattered stones from the surrounding grass and put them in their own, separate pile. If I found a stone which might go into either pile, we would discuss it: this was a serious matter!

Sometimes, even though the damage might be relatively small, Harry would dismantle a whole section of wall in order to strengthen it. The biggest, flattest stones went first and the wall would gradually build up; all the time we were aiming to have a level shelf. As Harry put in stones from his pile, so I would insert my smaller stones into the gaps, pushing and bashing them in with eight-year-old fingers that could easily fit into the tiniest spaces. The wall grew higher until our repair was level on either side with the existing wall; it was very satisfying!

There was one annual job to do. Each summer, Harry would completely dismantle a whole section of the wall of the top field. We put the stones in a heap to be used for the reconstruction later, but you had to be careful – there were a lot of stinging nettles down there! Where the lane continued round to the left at the top of Conway Road, Harry made a huge gap in the field wall so that, instead of following the lane round to go through the main field gate you could just walk straight through this gap. Once all the hay had been gathered from the field, we would spend a happy afternoon rebuilding the wall and the cows would once again be turned out to grass up there.

(Years later, I asked Harry about this yearly exercise.

"Oh, aye, that," he said. "Couldn't get th'orse and dray through the main gate. Not enough room to swing it round. Wi' that wall down we could just get straight back down the lane then through the Croft down into t'yard."

"You could have made a permanent gate there," I suggested. "Save doing it every year?"

"I could," he said.

Standing now by the playing fields at Marl Pits, I think about those field walls. They must have taken some dismantling. And I wonder what has become of all those stones . . .)

There was another on-going maintenance issue which Harry had to grapple with: drains. Out in the middle of the main field, which was the biggest and the one which led straight off the farmyard, Harry had trained a small spring to run through an old bath to make a drinking trough.

We talked about the it along with the stone walls. *(My sons were staggered at the things Harry and I found to talk about!)*

I pulled a face. "It was horrid down by that old bath, you know. All that muck and mud churned up. I was always sure the cows would be poisoned by that water in there."

"Poisoned? Nah, water were sweet enough. It collected in that bath, but it were running right through – always moving. It were good drinking water right enough, but it were never right, that drain. I had a go at it a few times. It always leaked. Some winters it were a right mess. There's a spring comes right off the moor and all the way down – you know, through that top field t'other side of the lane."

I did know. I remembered when we put drains in the top field too. Billy helped with that work.

"It were a big job that top field. Took a fair few days – do you remember that trench we dug?"

I certainly did – the mud! It was a lovely summer, the cows were out for the day on the moor, and I sat in the sunshine making a chain of buttercups while Harry and Billy worked on the drain.

It was interesting to watch Harry remember all this. "Had to take the cart up, we needed so much tackle. And then Billy fell in the ditch – remember that?" I did. In spite of the relatively dry weather, the trench for the new drain was wet and slippery. The brothers needed their wellingtons for the mud, but they had little grip and Billy, reaching for a spade, skidded spectacularly into the bottom of the trench and slid several feet flat on his back. Harry and I, initially speechless, then howled with laughter. Even Billy saw the funny side as he shook the mud from his curly hair.

Now, we laughed again. "It was like slow motion, I've never forgotten it!"

Harry chuckled along. "It were hard work that one. But we got it right. That field were never too wet after then."

(In 2020, I took a walk up into that top field. It wasn't the meadow I remembered, but it is still a

recognisable field. The grass is pretty wild now, it is hard to recall Billy bouncing along on a tractor pulling the baler, even harder to think of Diamond pulling a dray around up there. I skirted pools of water and whole areas of soft mud. The grass is more akin to marsh reeds in places. I shook my head: those field drains must have busted some time ago.)

Eleven

Hay-Making

Hay-making season was always a combination of great excitement and fun coupled with anxiety. There was lots to do, preparing the loft over the shippen and the Dutch barn, which both had to be completely swept, the barn in particular took a lot of work.

In the spring, we used to take Diamond with the small cart out into the fields for muck-spreading. This wasn't as unpleasant as it sounds and Harry kept that cart and a fork solely for this purpose. Needless to say, I didn't ride in this one!

After the last of the cows had been sent out to grass for the day, we would get busy, tramping up and down the various fields, the manure flying off the big fork, encouraging the grass to grow. This may have been an old-fashioned way of spreading fertiliser, but it certainly worked. Those fields produced grass as high as my waist in no time.

There was no romantic nonsense of apple-cheeked children running through long grass. Harry was quite firm that once the muck-spreading had taken place, the fields were out of bounds. He wanted the grass to grow strong and uniformly so that it could be cut evenly. And also so that we got every possible blade of grass – he didn't want to have to buy hay in as we got towards the end of the following winter.

But, of course, we were at the mercy of the weather and this particularly mattered once the grass was cut. The Spences would hire a mowing machine and driver to get this work done. That was a bit of excitement in itself – a machine at Springhill Farm! And a couple of days off for Diamond for once.

Now that the grass was cut, in long straight rows, fine weather was essential. (This is Rossendale, we're talking about!) I can remember one wettish early summer looking out of the high windows at school and worrying about the rain – what would we do if we couldn't get the hay in? I feared it would never dry out. The work it generated! To try to get this cut grass dry, Harry would work up and down the long rows turning the grass with a pitchfork. I couldn't help him, I couldn't even lift a pitchfork, never mind turn grass. And of course, once wet, the grass was itself heavy. Oh, it could be a nightmare.

Other years, we were more fortunate. In 1962 – or possibly 1963 – when I would be either eight or nine, there was a wonderful hay season with beautiful warm, clear days and, it turned out, it was the last year that Harry didn't have the hay baled. Looking back, it was like one of those nineteenth century oil paintings of horses with drays piled high with hay, golden colours with the odd hen clucking about.

Harry and Billy must have got through the morning milking very early. Billy said he'd put his alarm clock in a bucket so it made extra noise to wake him up! (I wonder if he did - I think about that every now and again!) By the time I got to the farm, the cows were already out for day and Diamond was out in the yard, wearing her harness ready for the dray. I don't think the dray was particularly heavy, it was just big and creaky: a long flat bed of wooden planks and it was quite wide too. It was kept under the awning just outside the shippen and was only used for its proper purpose on these relatively few days of hay-making. The rest of the time, Harry used it as a huge shelf for sacks of calves nuts, rolls of netting, hay rakes, ancient farm tools, rusting tins of nails, old pig troughs and anything else that couldn't immediately find a home.

Together, the brothers pulled the dray out into the yard and Billy ducked right underneath it – checking the wheels. Harry fastened Diamond between the shafts and Billy threw three or four pitch forks and a couple of hay rakes onto the dray. Two or three men I didn't know turned up and Mrs Spence, who was going to collect the eggs herself that day, arrived with sandwiches wrapped in waxy paper.

Mrs Spence was quite sharp with a couple of the men and then she turned to me.

"You listen to our 'arry and keep out of the way," she commanded. I nodded solemnly and Billy winked at me. We were good to go!

There were three distinct areas to be harvested, and that first day we managed the whole of one section – the two fields running right alongside the backs of houses on Newchurch Road, from Higher Cloughfold as far as what is now the entrance to the Marl Pits sports centre. It was very hot work, but (from my point of view at least) it was marvellous fun. These men had done this work before and were really quite skillful at getting mounds of loose hay onto the dray and making it stay there. The pitch forks flashed in the sun, up and down, poking and prodding to keep the load in shape and steady. Of course, bits were always sliding off. Billy took up position right on top as the hay piled higher and then, at some point, Harry called a halt. He threw a couple of ropes up to Billy, and they went up and over the whole load. Billy jumped down and we trundled back to the farm with our haul.

The next part of the job was to my mind the most memorable and I can see it in my mind's eye as if it were last week and not sixty years ago!

Diamond slowly pulled the dray about halfway down the yard, coming to a halt right alongside the building. Meanwhile, Billy went into the stable, nipped up that worm-ridden ladder into the hay loft and then opened a pair of doors right over the dray below. Pitch forks once again at the ready, the hay was transferred from the dray into the loft. I don't know how they did it, even though I was standing there watching. The hay itself was all loose, but there seemed to be some way of spearing it with a fork so that it stayed in a bundle and didn't just fly about. Billy and one of the other men were in the loft pulling the hay in, two were on the dray passing it up and Harry stayed on the ground, keeping Diamond steady and generally keeping things in order. Glen, of course, was going bananas on the end of his chain, but he shut up after a while.

Once the dray was cleared, we set off into the fields again. I must have gone home for lunch at some point, but the hay-making went on all day. I think we were all exhausted. At one point, Billy let me have some of his dandelion and burdock from a big brown bottle. It is not something I have ever drunk much, but whenever I do, I am straight back hay-making in the sunshine.

Eventually we called it a day, but of course, Harry and Billy still had the evening milking to do . . .

Baling hay wasn't nearly so exciting. You've seen one hay bale, you've seen them all. The baling machine was a very odd shape, it was bright red and was pulled by a blue tractor which, to my surprise, Billy drove. (Up to then it hadn't occurred to me that either he or Harry could drive.) When I arrived in the top field that year, work had already started. To my mind, the baler was incredibly quick, churning through the loose hay and popping out uniform rectangular bales already secured with strong twine. It may not in fact have been all that swift, but speed was not something one associated with Springhill Farm! It was certainly a whole lot quicker than pitchforks and a dray.

While Billy, bouncing up and down on the springy tractor seat, worked on producing the bales, Harry brought Diamond and the provin cart up into the field. He and I, at a far more sedate pace, set about collecting the bales of hay and transferring them back to the farm. Most of them went into the Dutch barn by the field gate. The compact hay in the bales made them deceptively heavy and, as I was to learn the hard way, the string was practically unbreakable and cut your hands. They were, of course, far easier to stack both in the cart and in the barn, but something was lost somehow. *(I suppose I am being romantic, baling must have been a much more efficient system.)*

If Harry had been lucky with the weather, there would now be time for a second harvest. He didn't do the whole acreage again, just parts of fields, which he would section off with electric fences to stop the cows getting in. The electric fences made me nervous. They consisted of a single, fat cable supported by stakes knocked into the ground at intervals. At one end was a big battery which hummed. I suppose the cable would be about three feet off the ground; Harry assured me that if a cow touched this electric fence it would give it a jolt – but it wouldn't kill it! I was never quite sure, but in all fairness, the farm wasn't littered with dead cows!

So it was back to muck-spreading again . . .

Every possible source of hay was utilised. The Upper Croft was really too small for any sort of machinery, so Harry actually scythed that little field. I don't think he got much off it, but he worked steadily and would get it done in a few hours. When the cut grass was fully dried out, I used to help him by carrying armfuls of hay into the small barn which stood in the corner. He used to say it was for emergencies. He scythed the edges of other fields too, we had to get every last scrap of hay, and, you know, I think we did.

Twelve

Nowadays

When we went to live in Higher Cloughfold, there were two shops, the Red Lion pub, Zion Baptist Church and a bus stop on either side of the road. After that, there was Springhill House, with a Lodge at the gate, a cluster of post-war prefabs, assorted cottages and houses which stretched along Newchurch Road in both directions. There were also houses part-way up Edge Lane and along the newly-named Conway Road. Then there was Johnny Barn auction mart, Springhill Farm and one other small farm much higher up Edge Lane.

Sixty years later, the place is still very recognisable. There have been changes, of course. The auction mart is no longer there, although the Johnny Barn name lives on, the original Baptist church building has been redeveloped but there is still a church on that site and the graveyard is still there, and there is now only one shop.

Other changes include the demolition of the prefabs, replaced by more permanent housing, and the erection of a crash barrier in front of the cottages opposite Springhill.

Strangely, it was the crash barrier that was an affront to my memory when I first saw it. Now, I barely notice it!

I was surprised to find that Mrs Smith's corner shop at the top of Peel Street had not only closed but been turned back into a house. These days you wouldn't realise it had ever been a shop, but when we lived in Higher Cloughfold it was a busy, thriving little place. Mrs Smith was a busy woman. There was pretty much always somebody in the shop and she also made up orders of groceries as she went along. She sold cigarettes, sweets and all manner of tinned and packaged goods, but she didn't sell fruit or vegetables and she didn't cut bacon or ham. Those were available at the other shop, run by Mr and Mrs McGrath.

Mrs Smith didn't have much of a till either. She kept a supply of scrap paper on her counter together with a biro, and no matter how many items were being bought she wrote them down and added them up carefully. What she certainly did have was a dog. This fox terrier was incredibly noisy. Thinking about it now, I am amazed she put up with it because it barked constantly at all the customers opening and shutting the shop door. One afternoon, when I was about nine, this dog bit me. I had gone in to buy some sweets. Mrs Smith asked what I wanted and as I pointed, the dog leapt up and grabbed at my finger. To this day, when I am cold, the scar where the dog's teeth scraped down my finger can still be seen.

I scurried back to the farm – Harry might know what to do. He did; he took one look and sent me home to "get summat done wi' it".

I didn't go in Mr and Mrs McGrath's shop nearly so much. Where Mrs Smith's was good-natured and bustling, the McGraths ran an altogether more restrained establishment. I suspect they were considerably older than Mrs Smith, although I didn't think of that at the time. When you're seven all adults are old!

Anyway, by the time I was nine they had left the business and it was taken over by the Pickles family. Things looked up and I used to go in the shop much more frequently. It is that shop which is still there now.

I never went to an auction at Johnny Barn, something I regret now. I don't think Billy would have wanted to take me, even though he worked there, but Harry might have gone with me. Knowing more about her now, it is not beyond the bounds of possibility that Mrs Spence would have been prepared to go. (I would have had to be very careful when I asked her though!) So, a little older perhaps, I might actually have got to see the famous Johnny Barn auction in action; as it was, I didn't. In those days it was a very busy place, with big cattle lorries and sheep with their faces poking through the sides of wagons. The auction house also owned fields, some of which bordered Springhill Farm and there were often bullocks grazing in the fields down near Waingate and in one of the top fields on the way to the tip.

Once, the Rossendale Hunt assembled on the Red Lion car park and spilled around the front of the building. We watched from the main gate of Springhill, it was tremendously exciting with lots of dogs milling about, horses, ponies and foot-followers all gathering before they set off up Edge Lane. It was the only time I have ever seen a woman ride side-saddle for real. I thought this lady looked marvellous with her skirt sweeping over the horse's flanks and just the toe of her riding boot peeping out.

Of course, I never went inside the Red Lion – in fact I have only ever been in there once, in 1993 just before my Granny's funeral service at Newchurch church.

Thirteen

Market Days

By the time I was nine, I used to go down to Rawtenstall by myself. It was no big deal, really, I just walked down Newchurch Road, almost always on the right-hand side, the same side as Springhill and, more usefully, the same side as the market.

The market was exactly where it is now, down at the bottom of the road with outside and inside stalls. A place of possibilities when you are nine with a sixpence to spend.

The outside stalls were mainly fruit and vegetables, I think, but there was one which sold purses and bags. One of my school friends bought a little purse there – it was made out of plastic shaped and decorated to be a cat's face and it had a zip over the top of the cat's head. You could get good sweets on the market too; I liked the toffee ones covered in icing sugar, but sometimes, for a change, I bought plums and custard ones which had a gritty coating of sugar.

One time, I bought a purse for my Mum for her birthday. I would have had extra money with me to buy that, it cost seven and six - three half crowns, which was a lot! The purse was bright red with a good clasp and she used it for years for her housekeeping money. (That purse survived through house removals, overcoats and shopping baskets, but one day it just disappeared. We ransacked the car, the house, the garden – but it never turned up.)

I rarely went into the indoor market. There were things like pies and bacon, rolls of cloth and towels, cages for budgies – not items on the shopping list of a little girl!

Once the market had been inspected, I was off to the library. As far as I can remember this was pretty much a straight walk from the market down Bank Street, but the layout of Rawtenstall town centre is so altered now that it may not have been quite how I recall. The library, of course, is the same – on the outside. In the early 1960s, the interior was all dark brown wood and shades of green paint and tiles. It was also hushed.

I loved it. I loved watching the ladies behind the counter running their fingers through the boxes of tickets when I returned my books, I loved the satisfying clunk of the date stamp showing me when I should return books I borrowed, I loved wandering along the shelves choosing books . . .

One Saturday morning when I was about ten, one of the library ladies came out from behind the counter.

"Look," she said, "we've got a new section for your age group, I think you might like it." And she showed me two bookcases over by the windows where the nursery children meet nowadays. This was a new concept for me. Prior to this very moment, there had been children's books and grown-ups' books. The idea of teenage reading was very new. Come to think of it, the whole idea of teenagers was pretty new. I was a bit troubled really and told the lady I was only ten. I can't remember what she said to this, but she seemed to think my reading ability would cope and suggested I should take a look. I did.

A new landscape presented itself. I can still remember the first book I chose from this new section, it was about an adventure on an island in the West Indies. (Of course, I had heard of the West Indies through Mr Kennedy and his cricket teams at school.) What I can't remember is the name of the book! It had very white paper and smaller type than I was used to and the plot seemed quite involved. I had to concentrate! But that library lady had been onto something – I never went back to the children's section.

(There is a small, amusing footnote to my life as a member of Rawtenstall library. In 2012, back after a gap of almost fifty years, I applied to rejoin. I explained to the woman at the desk that I had been a member but this had lapsed. I said that I thought I had last been there in 1964.

The woman consulted her computer. "You're not in the database," she said. It was almost an accusation. I thought of the brass-handled drawers of tickets and the clunky date stamp. Database? I'm not even sure the word existed in 1964. So no, I wasn't in the database – but I am now!)

Fourteen

Dancing in Bacup

The Farm wasn't the only distraction during the Easter holidays. The other great attraction took place on Easter Saturday in Bacup – the annual dance of the Britannia Coconutters. A vast amount has been written about this little troupe over the years; I believe university theses have even been based on the dancers and their origins.

However, leaving academia aside, the Coconutters are men with blacked-up faces wearing clogs and little skirts who dance from pub to pub in the streets of Bacup accompanied by a mournful little band which only plays two tunes. If this sounds implausible, it is – but when you are seven, running along the pavement with the dancers, it is the best fun ever!

Bacup is at one end of the Rossendale Valley and we didn't often go there, except to see a great uncle and his family who lived on New Line. But Easter Saturday was – and still is - a date not to be missed. My Mum danced along the pavements with the Coconutters when she was young, and I think it's quite possible my Granny did too.

(It is tremendously reassuring to know that the Coconutters are still there, just as they always were;

so much about Rossendale has changed, but they just keep on dancing and the tunes are just the same. The Coconutters and their black faces come under intense scrutiny from time to time. There are fierce arguments for and against the continuing tradition. Some say it is only a matter of time before they have to hang up their clogs; I wouldn't bet on it!)

The only other reason I ever had to go to Bacup was to learn to swim. I had lessons at the public baths there and I was taught crawl stroke. This was a really unhappy experience. At the end of the course of lessons, it was true that I could swim, but I never felt secure in the water and as a result I have never enjoyed swimming.

I wish now that I had re-learned at some stage, but the idea was never attractive after my experiences at Bacup swimming baths. Sometimes, I went with a friend to Haslingden baths, but my heart was never in it. There was a good vending machine with hot chocolate at Haslingden though!

Talk of swimming pools, however, brings me to Marl Pits.

In 2012, on a week-long visit to Rossendale, more or less to see if I would like to come back to live here, I went to the sports centre. I had feared that it would be hard, but actually the landscape is so utterly changed that it wasn't difficult at all.

The entrance to the sports complex, off Newchurch Road, is just about where the original gate to that field was. We didn't access the field from the road, and that gate was almost never used except once a year by a small lorry which delivered a mound of lime that Harry used as a fertiliser. There had been an old tree there too with a wooden sign hanging on it which said TRESPASSERS WILL BE PROSECUTED, or at least it would have done if all the letters had still been there.

I parked my rental car and pottered about. Springhill Farm, which would have been way over on the right, is no more of course and now trees and bushes completely obscure what was the entrance to the yard. It is so changed, it is a different place.

I wandered over past the rugby pitch in the general direction of the farm to an area which hadn't been developed. Water seeped round my feet, the ground was spongey – not boggy, but definitely wet. This, I realised with a jolt, must be where the bath-well was. I actually smiled. Harry never did get those drains right in this field!

Back over towards the buildings, I found a groundsman working at the side of one of the playing fields.

I explained I was visiting after a long time away.

"Did you know Harry Spence? He used to have the little farm over there."

"Oh, aye, Harry. Yes, I knew him – and his brother. They fell out. But I used to see Harry a fair bit, walking about you know."

"We used to come hay-making in the fields here," I said.

The groundsman was surprised. "It's quite wet round here," he said doubtfully, "I'm surprised if you got much hay."

I didn't pursue it – hay-making just seemed like another lifetime. But it was interesting that the rift between Harry and Billy was so well-known and remembered.

"It's bad today," the groundsman observed. "Bin raining."

"There's a spring comes up over there," I said, pointing to show him. "It's very small of course, but Harry used to have an old bath there to collect the water for the cattle to drink. It was quite effective. He did put field drains in sometimes. We did some much further up as well, in that field the other side of the lane to the council tip."

"Oof, you're going back a bit," the groundsman scratched his head. "There's no tip up there now. Not much left of the lane either – it's really just a path now."

I wandered on; I didn't need to worry about laying ghosts here, the place was empty of memory. I could have been anywhere.

Fifteen

Bobby Dazzler

At Easter in 1964, Springhill Farm took a cautious step into the twentieth century. I was ten by now and strode confidently up the yard at the start of the school holidays. I knew the milking would be in full swing, I was looking forward to seeing if Harry had any new calves – it was always a possibility at that time of year.

I reached the shippen door and stopped short. There was a funny noise – quite an insistent loud hissing, which had nothing to do with cows.

"What ...?" I looked at Harry.

"Milking machine," he said. "Makes a racket."

I was amazed. The shippen had been fitted with overhead metal pipes and there were various rubber hoses and milking tubes. The tubes had to be fitted to a cow's udder by hand but then worked by suction. The hissing was the air compression system and Harry could turn it on and off at a switch by one of the pollys.

(I suppose that the farm must have eligible for a grant, no way did Mrs Spence have money for this sort of investment!)

As far as I was concerned the real difference this automation made was speed. The milking sessions were now much quicker, and I couldn't chat to Harry in the way that I had before because he was always moving about - not sitting still for several minutes on his little stool. Billy wasn't around as much either; Harry could manage without the extra help now.

I have to smile. Once the milking machine routine was up and running, Harry bought four more cows. These four couldn't be housed in the main shippen, which was full, and so were put into another, smaller barn off the main yard. This barn was not linked to the shippen's system and so the newcomers had to be milked by hand! Dear Harry, a sucker for punishment . . .

It was all change about that time. Diamond was in foal and Harry wouldn't let her pull the provin cart to Rawtenstall any more. But apparently there was only so much automation Springhill Farm could manage at once; we would not be getting a tractor to replace Diamond - a black carthorse was hired for the duration. Harry didn't turn this horse out into the main field with the cows, he put it in the Upper Croft on its own – presumably because it wasn't his.

From time to time, the Upper Croft was used for this sort of segregation purpose. At one stage we had a young Friesian bull come to stay. It wasn't a friendly sort of animal. Harry actually wrapped a chain round the gate and was quite firm that I was not to go in that field.

"Not even if your hat blows in there."

Since I didn't wear a hat, this was nonsense, but I got the message!

"The bantams get under the gate," I pointed out.

"They'll mind themselves. It won't bother with them."

That bull got big quite quickly. I never did find out what it was doing with us, and one Saturday morning I found that it had gone.

The milking machines turned out to be the least of the changes at Springhill Farm in 1964. That year our fields were taken over to be turned into the Marl Pits sports complex. I can't speak of it coherently; I was just utterly bewildered. Huge machines were battering our land flat, digging out some areas, piling soil high in others, creating acres of mud – it was just awful. And it wasn't just our fields; the Johnny Barn fields went too, all churned up into a vast mess. Harry chained the field gate shut, we wouldn't be using it any more.

But, cows still have to milked, eggs still need collecting and somehow we soldiered on. The cows had to be taken up through the Croft and along Conway Road to graze up on the moor. We still had the top field too, so as the weather got colder Harry put them there for the day.

Diamond, and two sheep which had appeared from nowhere, had to make do with the Upper Croft. (Diamond's foal was sold as soon as it was old enough to leave her.)

I told Harry I would be leaving Newchurch school that summer. I would start at Bacup and Rawtenstall Grammar School in Waterfoot in September.

He nodded. "Have you told me mother?"

Mrs Spence? No, I hadn't told her.

"Here, take them eggs down and tell her," he said.

I gave Mrs Spence the eggs as usual; she started a new tray of six rows of six and then I told her about the grammar school.

Well! She was absolutely delighted! I was astonished – this was Mrs Spence who made me sit in silence, Mrs Spence who frowned on "big ideas", Mrs Spence who seemed to think I might get in our 'arry's way or even get chilblains.

She was thrilled – so thrilled in fact that she gave me a duck egg. I couldn't believe it.

The BRGS uniform was very smart and the first uniform I had ever had. I had a navy blue gymslip, a white blouse and tie, a cardigan and a blazer. Then, I had black leather shoes, a dark brown leather satchel and a beret. Marvellous.

In view of her enthusiasm, I thought I might earn a few Brownie points if I showed Mrs Spence this new outfit. (It never did any harm to be on the right side of her!)

I walked round from the back of Springhill, feeling a bit self-conscious, and met Mrs Spence just as she was coming down the steps from hanging out her washing. She looked me up and down.

"You'll do," she said. "Have you shown our 'arry?"

No, I hadn't. I had no intention of going up the yard dressed like this!

"Go and show him," she commanded. "And mind them shoes!"

I hovered uncertainly in the doorway of the shippen. I wasn't sure Harry would hear me over the noise of the milking machines, but equally I didn't want to risk getting splashed – or worse!

"Hello!" I shouted, "Hello! Harry!"

"Hello!" He suddenly appeared from between two cows down at the far end. He put a bucket down and walked up the length of the shippen towards me.

"I've come to show you," I said, shifting from foot to foot, feeling a bit silly somehow.

Harry smiled broadly. "Well now," he said, "aren't you a Bobby Dazzler!"

Sixteen

Sad News

For nearly thirty years, I knew nothing about Springhill or the farm. The house became a nursing home after we left, with horrid Lino floors where our lovely carpets had been, and the farm ticked along, same old, same old.

I suppose it was just on a back shelf of my memory, rarely recalled. And then, sometime in the early 1990s, I received a letter from my aunt – Dorothy, who had been Betty's friend. I lived in Hong Kong at that time and I can still picture myself opening this unexpected letter: Betty, Harry and Billy's only sister, had died. No. NO! She couldn't have died! She was only in her early sixties – far too young! I was distraught.

Dorothy didn't have many details herself, but she had thought I would want to know. Betty, it seemed, had married a cousin after Mrs Spence had died, but she and her husband then lived at Springhill farmhouse with the brothers. (It must have made a very odd household.) Of course, as a result of this news, it all came rocketing back to me. I wrote to Harry and Billy. They wouldn't reply (obviously) and I had to make up their address, but I was confident that providing the letter got as far as Higher Cloughfold, it would find them.

I left Hong Kong with my own family in 1992, coming back to England to live in a London suburb, but it wasn't until 2001 that I finally found myself back in Edge Lane.

After that first reunion, I went once more to the farmhouse, prising little bits of information out of Harry. On my second trip, his arthritis was noticeably worse.

"Got rid of the dog," he said. "It died."

I raised an eyebrow. "Died?" I must have sounded suspicious.

"I didn't kill it!" he protested. "Couldn't have killed it with these hands now."

Hmm. We moved on. He told me that Billy was now living in an old people's home, but he didn't know where and had no intention of finding out. I was a bit at a loss, I would have quite liked to see Billy. I also discovered that Harry had never been inside Springhill House. (Never!) He had never been to Clitheroe and when I likened it to Skipton, it turned out he'd never been there either. Had he ever left Rossendale?

Harry wouldn't ever tell me when his birthday was. As a child I had found this rather mysterious. After all, I told him when mine was! But he wouldn't budge. The nearest I could get him to tell me was that his birthday was "around Christmas". I began to think that it must be Christmas Day itself, but clearly he wasn't one for birthdays. Imagine my utter astonishment when, in October, 2003, I received a birthday card: In very shaky capital letters it reads

103

"OCT 14. HAPPY BIRTHDAY. HALF. CENTURY. SPRINGHILL." That's it. He didn't sign it – he didn't need to. Fancy him remembering, going to that effort. I was very touched.

I heard, via Dorothy, when Billy died. There was no word from Springhill farmhouse; it seemed the feud had gone on until the end. I was sad about Billy and, in spite of his animosity, I was sad for Harry too. His last remaining relative had now gone.

Then, in 2004, I received a letter from Mrs Earnshaw, the neighbour who had done Harry's shopping once he could no longer leave the house:

Margaret Earnshaw
7 Conway Road
Higher Cloughfold
Rawtenstall
Rossendale
Lancs BB4 7ST

25th July 2004

Dear Esther-Margaret

I am not sure whether you will know me, but Dorothy should remember me I am sure, my maiden name was Preston, I lived at the cottage 1 Edge Lane.
I am writing on behalf of Harry who received your card and photoes (sic) on the 22nd, at present he is in hospital, having suffered a very slight stroke, it has only affected his left arm and leg and has left them feeling heavy, he is still alright mentally and is very

well in himself, although, over the past years he has had limited mobility, and now is unable to walk, therefore he doubts he can look after himself and is coming to the conclusion a nursing home may be the best option, however there are other people to talk to before that decision is made.

I will let you know in due course what the outcome is going to be.

Yours sincerely

Margaret Earnshaw.

As good as her word, Mrs Earnshaw did indeed write again. It had proved impossible for Harry to go home to the farmhouse and after his stay in hospital, he had now gone to live at the Lumb Valley Care Home. Mrs Earnshaw had been very diligent: she had visited sixteen care homes before she was satisfied that this one would be the right choice!

Getting to Lumb on public transport was a bit of a stretch, but needs must and I visited Harry there as soon as I could.

"You found me then," he said. He was sitting in a wheelchair, his hair newly washed.

"You knew I would!"

"Aye, I suppose I did."

"I heard Billy died."

"Yes. I didn't go t'funeral. Well, I couldn't with these legs. But I wouldn't have gone any road."

He didn't actually say good riddance, but it hung in the air. I moved quickly on, asking him about the farmhouse. "Can't go back. I knew as soon as I fell with this stroke that I wouldn't be going back. Couldn't do them stairs any road. Never left before."

"Do you miss it?"

"No. It were just an 'ouse." (I thought this was quite remarkable since he had literally lived there all his life.)

"So will you sell it now?"

"T'int mine to sell."

"Well whose is it?" I was astonished – there wasn't anybody else!

"Mother left it to Betty. She had a note put in that I could live there long as I wanted. So I stayed put.

"Betty had a bathroom put in upstairs." (I bet she did. Thank goodness!) "Big enough to swing a horse and cart. Don't know why she had it made so big. Any road, Betty died without a will, so her husband got th'ouse. And then he died without a will too, so his niece or somebody owns it. Lives in Norfolk."

"But all the time you were allowed to live there under the terms of your mother's will?"

"That's right. But I've had to leave now."

It didn't really surprise me – what a mish-mash. I looked around; Harry now lived in more comfort than he had in his entire life. It was the last time I saw him.

He died in January, 2008, only days after his eighty second birthday (which wasn't on Christmas Day at all, it was in early January). I was "nearly fifty five"; he had been my friend for almost fifty years. I telephoned the care home and spoke to the manager, who was actually very upset about Harry's death herself.

"He was quite a favourite here," she said. "We shall miss him."

I think it's really sad that Harry didn't have children of his own. He didn't even have nephews or nieces, and yet he was a man who loved children, understood them, was happy to have them about. I was never under his feet, never mithered him. He kept a photograph of my sons on his mantelpiece along with a little picture of Betty. I feel very proud about that.

Author's Acknowledgement

The story of Springhill Farm and my childhood in Rossendale has been a labour of love, but of course I could not have written it without the help and encouragement of everyone who has urged me to record it.

In particular, I must thank David and Jane Upton, who have indulged my insistence on looking at cows during our hostel holidays. It was from the conversations that this generated that the idea of a memoir evolved. Subsequently, they have offered advice, support and enthusiasm – all essential to the creative process. Additionally, David has been instrumental in shaping the finished product!

My thanks also to John Mansergh, at the corn merchants, who provided me with some insight into the operation of the Rawtenstall business and shared his memories of the Spence family.

As always, my questionable technical abilities have been patiently refined by my son George who has steered this book into print.

After leaving Canon Slade Grammar School in Bolton, Esther-Margaret Hood trained as a journalist on the Fylde coast, working first as a reporter on the Lytham St Annes Express before going on to the nearby Evening Gazette in Blackpool as a sub-editor. After extensive travels and working abroad, she lived for a while in Hong Kong – where she started a family – before returning to the UK to live in London.

Esther-Margaret now lives in Rossendale.

Printed in Great Britain
by Amazon